This Risen Existence

Paula Gooder is a freelance writer and lecturer in biblical studies. She is Canon Theologian of Birmingham Cathedral, a Reader in the Church of England, and a member of General Synod.

Her numerous books include *The Meaning is in the Waiting: The Spirit of Advent* (Canterbury Press), *Lentwise: Spiritual Essentials for Real Life* (Church House Publishing), and *Exploring New Testament Greek: A Way In* (SCM Press).

She lives in Birmingham.

This Risen Existence

The Spirit of Easter

Paula Gooder

CANTERBURY
PRESS

Norwich

© Paula Gooder 2009

First published in 2009 by the Canterbury Press Norwich
Editorial office
108-114 Golden Lane
London EC1Y 0TG

Canterbury Press is an imprint of Hymns Ancient and
Modern Ltd (a registered charity)
St Mary's Works, St Mary's Plain,
Norwich, NR3 3BH, UK

Fourth impression 2021

www.canterburypress.co.uk

The R. S. Thomas poem 'Suddenly' is from Collected Poems:
1945–1990, 2000, and is reproduced by permission of Orion Books

Scripture quotations are from the New Revised Standard Version of
the Bible, copyright 1989 by the Division of Christian Education of
the National Council of the Churches of Christ in the USA. Used by
permission. All rights reserved.

British Library Cataloguing in Publication data

A catalogue record for this book is available
from the British Library

ISBN 978-1-85311-996-5

Typeset by Regent Typesetting, London
Printed and bound in Great Britain by
CPI Group (UK) Ltd, Croydon, CR0 4YY

For my dear friend Toni, who has,
on various occasions, been to me
the Spirit of Resurrection
when I needed it most.

CONTENTS

HOW TO USE THIS BOOK

This book is in some ways self-indulgent. Easter is one of my favourite times of the year and Resurrection one of the pillars of my faith. Yet many years I find myself disappointed. We work our way through Lent, reflecting deeply on issues of life and faith and, at last, arrive at Easter Day, when so often we stop our study and carry on as before. Many people read Lent books, some of which explore Jesus' journey to the cross but then stop just before the resurrection or, occasionally, mention the resurrection in their last chapter. I have for many years longed for a book that would take me on a journey through Easter to Ascension Day and Pentecost, which would allow me to think more deeply and seriously about what the resurrection means to me and the way in which I live my life. (Such a book might also allow me to rectify the fact that I never did quite finish that Lent book I began six weeks ago!)

In the end, I decided that the only thing to do was to write my own Easter book, which could accompany me on a journey through the stories and ideas about resurrection we encounter in the Bible, and to ask what living a resurrection life might mean. So this book is largely self-indulgent, but I hope not entirely so. If you, like me, have wanted to travel more deeply into what Jesus' rising from the dead really means, then I hope this book might be a helpful companion on your journey.

One of the challenges of writing an Easter book is how to apportion the chapters. Should Mark's Gospel get more or less space than Matthew's Gospel? How much room should Paul get? In the end, I decided to choose 42 passages which, if you opt to read this book between Easter and Pentecost, will give you six a week for seven weeks (one a day with one day off per week). You may of course not choose to read the book after Easter, or not solely after Easter, or not as a book of daily readings, and in that case you can decide for yourself what to read when.

You might like, before you begin, to decide how you want to go about considering the resurrection. One option is to follow the order I have put down (the resurrection in the Gospels, Paul, other Epistles, then the ascension, then Pentecost); another is to mix up the readings a bit more. If, for example, you know that you find the writings of Paul hard or, indeed, that you have a preference either for Paul's theology or the narratives of the Gospels, you might like to intersperse your readings from the Gospels with those from Paul. In this way you can reflect on the two side by side, which can be an interesting and helpful thing to do.

Most sections begin with a short passage from the New Testament which forms the basis of my reflection with a suggestion for a longer passage, if you would like to read further. Occasionally there is only the short passage because the longer context has been explored in either the previous or the subsequent section (or both).

On putting things in and leaving things out

One of the greatest challenges of writing a book like this is not so much what to put in as what to leave out. I had covered most (though not all) of the Gospel narratives about resurrection but then faced the challenge of how to select passages from Paul, Acts and the rest of the New Testament for the sections on the resurrection in the Epistles, the ascension and Pentecost. In the end I chose what I think are the most important passages then halved them, then shaved off a few more, until I was left with the ones included in this book. If I wrote this book again I might make different choices (and no doubt many of you would have chosen different passages as well) and so I offer this selection as a snapshot of what I thought were helpful passages at the time of writing.

In a similar vein, there is much, much more to say about the passages than I have said here. In the end I restricted myself to one major focus (with a few exceptions) per passage. This will inevitably mean that I have missed some crucially important points – and maybe included others that you might not have put in. I did this consciously because my aim in writing this book is to produce a series of reflections that are more suggestive than conclusive, more thought-provoking than exhaustive. I don't want to have the last word (or anything approaching the last word) but to frame some initial thoughts that might help you find your own words about the resurrection and our life in Christ.

The alert reader will notice that I haven't anywhere discussed the question of the historicity of the resurrection. The reason for this is very simple – I don't think it's the most important question to ask. This may sound surprising and I don't intend it to be. What I mean is that in the latter half of the twentieth century this was one of the only questions ever asked about the resurrection. The result was an almost impossible stand-off between those who said yes, it was historical, and those who said it wasn't, which, over time, led to a discomfort with talking about the resurrection at all. There is very little that can be added to the debate about historicity. The resurrection cannot be proved to be historical, but it would also be hard to disprove it. What we can do, however, is to ask what it *meant* to the earliest Christians and also what it might mean to us today. This is the major focus of my reflections in this book. If you wish to reflect further on questions of historicity, then you will need to look elsewhere and after the introduction I have made suggestions of a few books for further reading that might help you if you are interested in this area.

In a similar vein, I have also opted to take belief about the end times at face value. Although many Christians today prefer not to talk about the end of the world, perhaps because it seems so distant and unlikely, the New Testament writers were adamant in their belief that it would happen. We can only really understand resurrection if we also assume a belief in the end times. Remove the end of the world and much New Testament theology becomes illogical. Whatever your own beliefs on the subject, we have to take a step into the New Testament writers' world in order to comprehend what they were talking about. Part of that world was believing in the end times and we need to assume this outlook if we wish to talk about how the New Testament writers understood the resurrection.

Some main features of New Testament scholarship that I have also opted not to discuss in this book are questions of authorship, date and purpose of writing. These are vital questions but, in my view, are ground clearing or foundational questions which allow us to ask both what the texts meant then and what they mean now. In study books on the New Testament, it can happen that these 'pre' questions are asked in full and then the process of interpretation stops before questions of meaning are raised. In this book I have decided to cut out most of the 'pre' questions (since these are widely, and well asked elsewhere) and to concentrate instead on the questions of meaning. As a result, I shall refer to Mark as the author of Mark's Gospel and John and the author of the fourth Gospel – and so on – not because I am unaware of the issues surrounding authorship but because I am using this as shorthand in order to get us more quickly to the text itself. This also holds true of the Epistles. I am fully aware of debates about the authorship of Colossians and Ephesians, or of 1 Peter, but this book does not aim to adjudicate on who wrote what, when and where. If I began to do that then we would have little time to explore the resurrection. The only exception to this rule is the book of Hebrews which, though attributed to Paul in Christian tradition, mentions no author in the book itself. As the author remains anonymous in Hebrews, I shall treat him as anonymous here too.

I will also be talking about the different Gospel accounts of resurrection (calling them Mark's account, Matthew's account and so on). This is not meant to imply that Mark made his version up, or that Matthew is playing fast and loose with the details. All it recognizes is that the intricate art of weaving together a narrative, reflecting on it and drawing our attention to its significance is a task that each Gospel writer did differently and with different results. Again, questions of how their accounts relate to what actually happened are not our concern in this book.

Resurrection: A reflection

One of the challenges for understanding the resurrection is working out what resurrection meant to a first-century Jewish audience and how this should affect the way in which we think about it today. In order to help you to think about this further I have written an extended reflection on resurrection, what it meant, what it means and how that affects the way in which we live out our lives. Some people will find it to be a helpful lens through which to read the reflections on individual passages; others may find it overly complex and theological. Again how – or whether – you read it is up to you. If you would rather get into the exploration of the biblical stories straight away then do that and skip the introduction entirely. You can of course read it later – or indeed not at all – if that it more helpful.

The R. S. Thomas poem that begins the Introduction also functions as a different kind of lens through which we can read the accounts and descriptions of resurrection. My theological musings provide one kind of lens but the poem 'Suddenly' provides another, inner lens, which helps us to see this risen Christ whom we worship not with our eyes only but with the whole of our being.

Introduction

RESURRECTION

A Reflection

Suddenly

As I had always known
he would come, unannounced,
remarkable merely for the absence
of clamour. So truth must appear
to the thinker; so, at a stage
of the experiment, the answer
must quietly emerge. I looked
at him, not with the eye
only, but with the whole
of my being, overflowing with
him as a chalice would
with the sea. Yet was he
no more there than before,
his area occupied
by the unhaloed presences.
You could put your hand
in him without consciousness
of his wounds. The gamblers
at the foot of the unnoticed
cross went on with
their dicing; yet the invisible
garment for which they played

was no longer at stake, but worn
by him in this risen existence.

R. S. Thomas

Introduction

'Resurrection' is one of those words that always gives me the sneaking sense that I haven't really understood it. The feeling probably reaches back to my childhood, to the time before I realized that Jesus being risen from the dead and Jesus' resurrection were, in fact, the same thing. Whenever people talked about resurrection I assumed that it was something he did in addition to rising from the dead, though I could never work out what it might be. Then one glorious day I finally realized that resurrection was not as complicated as I thought and that it referred to Jesus rising from the dead, something which – oddly enough – seemed much easier to comprehend.

Nevertheless, the older I get the more I wonder whether my childhood self was in fact right and that resurrection is indeed more complicated. Of course, it refers to Jesus rising from the dead, but what is harder to understand is what this meant and continues to mean. On the simplest of levels Jesus' resurrection is straightforward good news – Jesus was dead; now he is alive. This simple but mind-blowing fact remains at the heart of the resurrection, but there is more to it than even that. Jesus' resurrection points us to a new way of looking at the world, a new way of being that changes who we are and how we live in the world. This opening reflection on resurrection explores a few of the key themes and attempts to capture some of the profundity of what believing in the resurrection might mean and what difference it might make to the way in which we live day to day.

Resurrection and new life

One of my favourite times of the year is spring. I love that feeling of the stirrings of new life that arises when first the tiniest spring flowers like snowdrops or aconites fight their way through the winter frosts, to be followed by crocuses, daffodils and apple blossom. Our local park has bank upon bank of crocuses and when I see them the biting wind feels less cold, the rain less endless and I start looking forward to warmer times and new life. On one level nothing has changed but on another it feels as though I have been granted permission to look forward to sunnier, warmer days.

There is something in the human psyche that responds to new life. Many people will pause to coo over a baby, a puppy, a kitten, in fact anything new-born. There are many scientific explanations of why we are so drawn to 'newness' but part of it must be that it gives us a sense of hope, of life beyond the grim realities of the everyday, of a future. In some ways, the resurrection of Jesus chimes in with this response to new life. Just as spring flowers intimate that winter is passing and summer is round the corner, so also Jesus' resurrection points us to the fact that the old order is passing and new creation is just about to happen.

There is a problem, however, with the analogy between Jesus' resurrection and spring flowers that we should not overlook. Those crocuses I love so much will die before summer has even arrived and will only have new life once more the following spring. Spring flowers suggest resurrection to us but only partially. The major difference between their rising to new life and Jesus' rising is that their new life is cyclical, interwoven with death, whereas Jesus' is not. Jesus rose to new life and will never die again.

When teaching in theological college, I would regularly get into arguments with my students over how unique Jesus' resurrection was. The conversation would go something like this. I would say, 'Jesus' resurrection was entirely unique, nothing like it had ever happened before, nor afterwards.' Without fail, someone would respond, 'Ah, but what about the widow of Nain's son in Luke 7.11–17 or Lazarus in John 11.1 –44?' And tension would rise in the room, since there is nothing a student enjoys more than proving their lecturer wrong. I maintained then, and still maintain now that my original statement is correct. The difference between what happened to Jesus and what happened to Lazarus is vast because just like the spring flowers Lazarus died again, and awaits another resurrection. Jesus did not die again, nor ever will; Jesus rose not to the same life – as Lazarus did – but to a different life in which death no longer features. Technically, what happened to Lazarus was not resurrection (rising to a new eternal life) but revivification (rising to a renewed old life). It is a picky point, but an important one and begins to open up the question of the 'something more' of the resurrection. Jesus' resurrection is more than just that he was dead and now is alive, since this could be said of Lazarus and many others who were miraculously raised in the Bible. What is 'more' about Jesus' resurrection is that he will never die again.

Resurrection and the end times

That is not all, however. There is even more to Jesus' resurrection than that. Although not every Jew in the first century believed in life after death, many of those who did believed in a bodily resurrection that would happen at a dramatic moment in the future when God would intervene in the world and return the kingdom to Israel. It was, they believed, at this point that the dead would be raised and that a time of peace and prosperity would begin. The resurrection would herald a new world order in which Israel would be freed from her enemies and would live in peace and prosperity. To a lot of Jews living at the time of Jesus, believing that a resurrection had happened would have meant believing that the end times – when all this would happen – had already started.

No wonder, then, the earliest disciples struggled to get their heads around Jesus' resurrection. Jesus had risen from the dead but no one else had; Jesus had risen from the dead but the world was, apparently, no different from the way it had been before: the Romans still occupied Palestine, the poor were still poor, Israel still downtrodden. A lot of the New Testament writers made sense of this by seeing Jesus' resurrection as a radical and transforming event which changed the world now. For them the 'something more' of Jesus resurrection was a belief that the end times had already started. For them, Jesus' resurrection signalled far, far more than a dead person living; it marked the start of a whole new way of being. The end times had begun, but not in their entirety; new creation sprang forth but still waited for fulfilment.

I heard one of the best ways of describing this not in a theology book but in a BBC drama, *The Second Coming,* which was televised in 2003. The play, written by Russell T. Davies, was about a character, Steven Baxter, who discovered he was the Son of God. In many ways it was disappointing and unsatisfying, but there was a brilliant scene when someone described the moment of revelation when the world recognized that Steve was the Son of God. She said that it was like a slice of one day being displaced into another: 'the event happened Thursday evening and there's a great big chunk of Tuesday in the middle.' Odd though this may sound, this is possibly one of the best descriptions of the displacement of time that took place at Jesus' resurrection that I've ever come across. Jesus' resurrection was a slice of end times, occurring about 2,000 years ago. More importantly even than that, the event of the resurrection continues to allow us to experience a slice of end times now.

As a result, the world is as it always was with its wars, heartache, poverty and oppressions, but with glimmers of end times perfection. In the midst of conflict and aggression, we can, from time to time, taste moments of reconciliation and of compassion. Occasions when the parent of a murdered son can forgive his killers, when a community can rise against the gangs that terrorize it and make it a better place, when we can rise above the petty arguments that spoil our human relationships are, for me, all a slice of the end times now. Some are dramatic world-changing occasions; others are small and apparently insignificant. Some affect whole nations and continents; others one or two individuals. The occasions may only be momentary and we quickly move back into the harsh reality of the everyday, but their effects linger, suggesting that new creation is possible and that transformation can happen.

As so often, C. S. Lewis put his finger on this beautifully in *The Lion, the Witch and the Wardrobe*, where he talks about Narnia, under the spell of the White Witch, being in a state that was 'always winter and never Christmas'. For years, I thought that this was wrong – surely he meant always winter and never spring – didn't he? I now see that he was right. When the spell of the White Witch was broken by Aslan's return to Narnia, the first sign of it was Father Christmas, then the melting of snow and finally the full blossoming into spring. If we use a similar analogy, we now live in the period between the advent of Father Christmas and the full melting of the snow – spring is on its way and we see signs that it is coming, but the full blossoming of the world as God yearns for it to be is a way off.

Belief in the resurrection is an act of rebellion against the evil, corruption and oppression that can so easily swamp us. Believing in the resurrection can be a refusal to accept that the world is as it is, that it can never change and that we must accept it simply as it is. Believing in the resurrection allows us to see the world with a long view, a perspective that looks backwards to the resurrection and forwards to the end times, recognizing traces of resurrection and end times in what is happening now. Believing in the resurrection can and should transform not only how we view the world, but how we live in it. We should become people in whom others can see new life, and people who introduce that new life wherever the world is stultifying and life-denying. Resurrection makes a difference not only to Jesus and the earliest disciples but also to us, as we live out our lives day by day.

Resurrection and life after death

One of the odd problems of talking about bodily resurrection is that it can be immensely distressing for people who are bereaved. If you ask people what they believe about what will happen to them – or to their loved ones – after death, they do not say 'bodily resurrection'. Although there is no single view about what happens after we die, most people would say that the souls of the dead are in heaven with God and that we will join them when we die. It is important to many people to feel that their loved ones are with God, safe in the heavenly realms, protected from all the harm that surrounds our human existence. Current research into first-century Jewish and New Testament understandings of resurrection seems to contradict this and to suggest that the key feature is in fact a bodily

resurrection to a renewed earth. As N. T. Wright so strik-
ingly puts it in his book, *The Resurrection of the Son of
God,* this is a belief in life *after* 'life after death': we die
and have a temporary existence from which we will be
raised to a new bodily life.

The problem, of course, is that when someone is bereaved it is incredibly difficult – and insensitive – to
suggest to them a new theological idea. Add to this the
problem that the grief of bereavement lasts a long time
and we can never know which sensitive spot in others,
or indeed in ourselves, we will hit when we stray into the
area. What then should we do? It is tempting to suggest
the well-tried solution of ignoring the issue and talking
about something nice and unchallenging instead. Ultimately, this is unsatisfying, however, and there is, I think,
a hunger to talk more about life after death and what it
means – so long as we do it well and sensitively. It often
feels as though the Church only tells you what you are
not allowed to believe about life after death and leaves
the rest to you, only speaking again when you have got
it wrong. What then can be said that is not too stretch-
ing but which does justice to the biblical idea of resurrection? There are two answers that are worthy of further
exploration.

The first is that no change to the common view is nec-
essary, we simply need to bolt resurrection onto the end
of what is already held to be true. There are texts, like
Daniel 12.2 for example, which seem to imply that the
dead lie in the earth until the moment of resurrection;
there are others, however, which speak of the souls of the
dead being in heaven right now. A particularly interesting
example of this is 1 Enoch 22.1–4 (a non-biblical text,
written roughly 300 years before Christ), which mentions
different areas of heaven in which both the wicked and
the righteous are kept until the day of judgement. They

stay in heaven awaiting the day of judgement and then are raised from the dead. This is not a far cry from what many people believe today; it simply weaves resurrection into what they already think.

Another answer is to reflect a little about the nature of time and to recognize that earthly time and heavenly time are not the same, as the Bible acknowledges on more than one occasion (see for example Psalm 90.4: 'For a thousand years in your sight are like yesterday when it is past, or like a watch in the night'). Add to this the belief that the resurrection of Jesus has collapsed time into itself so that the end times have already begun in the present, implying that the new earth and new heaven, resurrection and judgement might have both happened *and* not happened all at the same time (but don't ask me to explain how!). Then, mind-blowing though it may seem, the dead may already have been raised on the last day while we wait for its arrival.

Ultimately, we have to acknowledge that no one knows what will happen after death. The biblical and extra-biblical (that is, Jewish and Christian texts written at a similar time or later than the Bible but not included in the Bible) attempts to understand what happens are simply that – attempts. And though there are striking elements that many people seemed to believe in (resurrection, judgement etc.), there are striking differences as well (such as whether the souls of the dead are in heaven or sleeping in the dust of the ground before resurrection, and whether everyone will be raised or just the righteous). It is not for nothing that N. T. Wright's and Alan Segal's hefty books on the subject (see Further Reading on p. 000) are so long: an exhaustive treatment of the variety of possibilities requires a lot of space. We can say nothing with absolute certainty about life after death but we do need to carry on exploring it, in all its ambiguity, lack of clarity

and uncertainty. It is after all one of the theological ideas
that many people are desperate to talk about.

Resurrection and us

In some ways resurrection can seem remote from what we
do day to day. It feels abstract and far removed from our
lives; it's all very well talking about it but what difference
will it make to me as I go to work, do the school run or
chat with my friends? The apostle Paul's answer to this
would be that it makes all the difference in the world –
who you are and how you do your work or the school run
or how you chat with your friends is completely different
as a result of the resurrection.

In order to understand what Paul is talking about we
need to think a little bit about corporate and individual
identity. We live in a world that thinks, almost exclusive-
ly, in terms of individual identity. The common usages
of Descartes' famous saying, which translates into English as 'I think therefore I am', puts a lot of emphasis on
the pronoun – 'I think, therefore I am' – which reminds
me of a brilliant joke that I heard the late, great John
O'Donohue tell. Descartes was in a pub having a drink
and the barman came up to him to ask him if he would
like another drink. He refused. The barman pressed him
and Descartes paused and then said, 'I think not' . . . at
which point he disappeared. The point of the saying (and
of the joke) is that individual existence is everything. If
Descartes did not think, he did not exist. This idea would
be almost incomprehensible for Paul and the people who
lived in the first century.

Desmond Tutu, the great Archbishop and political act-
ivist, is credited with a type of theology that would make
much more sense to Paul than our own individualism.
This is often called 'Ubuntu theology' and draws on the

African understanding of interconnectedness. For Tutu, Descartes' adage needs adapting to 'I am human and therefore I belong' or 'I am because you are'. It is interesting that very young children also seem to understand this. When one of my daughters was younger, she was asked in a playgroup to draw a picture of herself. She sat very carefully drawing for much longer than the rest of her friends and finally came to show me the results of her artwork. There on the page was a carefully drawn picture of me, my husband, and both our daughters. I said to her 'Oh that's nice, you drew us all, but you only need to draw you.' She looked back at me and said, 'But this is me . . . me and my family.' At that stage, she saw herself almost entirely in terms of her family.

Throughout the Bible we find examples of the way in which the biblical authors thought more corporately than they did individually. One prime example is in the keeping of the law. Christians often misunderstand Hebrew attitudes to the law because we think so individually. A popular assumption is that a Jew thought that doing what is required by the law would bring him or her salvation. This cannot be the case. A Jew is a Jew because they are born Jewish; they cannot become more or less Jewish by doing or not doing something. If one Jew contravenes the law, he or she is still a Jew – maybe a bad Jew – but a Jew nevertheless. The point about observance of the law is not the salvation of an individual but of the nation as a whole. If the nation as a whole keeps the law, the covenant will be intact and God will save them from their enemies. The logic of the covenant is predicated almost entirely on corporate identity. If the whole nation is faithful, then the whole nation will be saved.

It is an interesting example of how bound into individualism we are that, often, when I have explored this with a group, someone will ask what proportion of the nation needs to keep the law for the whole nation to be deemed to be faithful. Again the answer is that this is a very individualistic way of thinking about it. Faithfulness – or lack of it – is a whole national characteristic not just that of an individual. How the nation behaves together, in relationship with one another and in relationship with God is vital. A corporate way of viewing the world recognizes that how the Israelites behave as a whole is important and that attitudes and actions are infectious for good or ill. In a sense, this is what was going on when Abraham bartered with God about the survival of Sodom. The story, found in Genesis 18.23–33, features a conversation between God and Abraham about how many righteous people were needed in Sodom to ensure that God did not destroy it. Abraham began with 50 and worked down to ten; God assured him that he would not destroy Sodom if he could find ten righteous people. The fact that Sodom was then destroyed implies that there weren't even ten righteous people. The point of that is that with ten righteous people it was still possible for righteousness to infect the whole, fewer than ten would make that very difficult.

What this seems to indicate is that groups (nations, cities, work places and churches, to name but a few) can have personalities just as individuals can. For example, there are some workplaces that are much easier to work in than others because the ethos or atmosphere is positive and encouraging, whereas in other places it is very hard because the atmosphere is difficult and unhappy. I've certainly been to meetings where the atmosphere was so difficult that it was hard to get anything done at all. This is an example of corporate identity where the attitude of a group as a whole becomes more powerful than that of any of the individual members. It is possible to change group identity but, as in the Abraham story, you need a

committed and determined group of people to infect the
whole with a different way of being.

I am not arguing that we should give up individualism
and attempt to embrace corporate identity again; I'm not
sure that would be either possible or desirable. What I
am suggesting is that there are insights from the corporate way of viewing the world that are vital for our comprehension of some pieces of the New Testament, and
resurrection is one of them. Much of Paul's understanding about Christian identity is based on Jesus' death and
resurrection, and on being 'in Christ'. This is something
that we will explore further in the actual studies from the
Bible (particularly the Pauline chapters) but it is worth
setting it out here briefly in the light of everything I have
said so far.

The apostle Paul thought that Jesus' resurrection had
not only transformed Jesus (from death to life) and time
(bringing the end times into the present) but also us. This
is a view that only really makes sense when we think corporately. In Romans 5—6, Paul talks about Adam and
Christ. When he talks about Adam in these passage he has
in mind corporate identity, so before Christ our corporate
identity was shaped by Adam and his marred relationship with God. The predominant ethos of humanity, Paul
argues, was one of disobedience and imperfect relationship with God. The only way to escape from our identity
in Adam was by dying. When Jesus died, he made a way
of escaping from identity in Adam and by rising again he
opened up a new identity, a Christ identity shaped, not by
Adam and who he was, but by Christ and who he was.
Our baptism marks that pattern of dying and rising with
Christ which allows us a new corporate identity now infected, not with Adam's imperfections, but with Christ's
perfections. If we are 'in Christ' then we have a new identity, a Christ identity, which involves viewing the world

as Christ did and acting in the world like Christ. In Paul's view we cannot be 'in Christ' and still be the same people we were before. Everything about who we are, what we think and what we do is now infected with Christ and, as a result, our lives should be entirely transformed.

Thus, the way in which we do the school run, go to work, chat with our friends and so on will be infected with 'Christ-likeness', marked by love, by lack of concern about status, by putting others before ourselves, by breathing new life into situations of despair and so on. Being 'in Christ' affects every aspect of our lives – even the most mundane of tasks. In recent years the popular acronym WWJD or 'what would Jesus do?' has come close to this kind of ethic, though not entirely. WWJD requires us to imitate Jesus (which is a great start). Living resurrection lives, however, requires us to go a step further. We are called to imitate Jesus but we are called even more to be transformed by him, to find our old self transformed into a new Christ-like self.

The problem, of course, is the impossibility of this calling. We so often fail in our vocation to be Christ-like. This is where we return to the notion of 'glimmers of end times' now. We cannot hope ever to become perfect Christ-like people overnight. Even a whole lifetime of the faithful living out our lives in Christ will leave us with a pale imitation of what our lives could be. This is not something that should make us feel bad but reassured. Jesus' resurrection opens up possibility. Whenever and wherever moments of generosity, selflessness and humility occur, where there could have been only greed, selfishness and pride, we are called to notice such moments and celebrate them, and when they do not occur to strive to bring them about.

Resurrection, ascension and Pentecost

Resurrection is not complete, however, without the ascension and Pentecost. The death, resurrection and ascension of Jesus and the sending of the Holy Spirit all come together as a seamless whole. The progression is simple but vital. Jesus' death and resurrection transform us and allow us to become the people that God wants us to be, but the ascension and Pentecost are equally important. Ascension is one of those sadly overlooked feasts of the Church. Often we are not too sure how to celebrate it. If we ignore it, however, we lose a vital link in the chain that runs from Good Friday to Pentecost Sunday. The resurrection offers us transformation in Christ, the ascension gives us the motivation to act and Pentecost the ability to do it.

Many human beings are, in all honesty, fundamentally lazy. If someone is doing something already, most people will leave it to them. The reason why the ascension was vital was that if the risen Christ had not ascended into heaven and was still on earth proclaiming the good news, healing the sick and befriending the poor and oppressed, then most of us would leave this work to him. We would become passive recipients of his ministry rather than active proclaimers of his message. After the resurrection, once they had grasped what had happened to Jesus, the disciples were in danger of slipping back into their previous form of existence. What they most needed was a vacuum, and this is what the ascension provided, a space that could only be filled if they picked up the challenge and took it on.

The resurrection and ascension, however, were of no use without Pentecost, because no matter how great the void left by Jesus at the ascension, the disciples were unable to act on their own. The sending of the Spirit gave them the ability to do what otherwise they were incapable

of doing. Filled with the Spirit they were able to comprehend the significance of the resurrection and to understand that Jesus' ascension and command to proclaim the
gospel sent them out into the world but, most important
of all, the Spirit gave them the ability to do as Jesus commanded. Beyond their human limitations, fears and anxi-
eties, the Spirit-filled disciples were at last able to do all
that Jesus asked.

This four-link chain then – death, resurrection, ascension and sending of the Spirit – is the underpinning of our
Christian existence. What difference does it make to our
lives today? The answer, it seems to me, is every possible
difference. A life lived in the acknowledgement of resurrection, ascension and Pentecost is one that cannot remain unchanged. We are called to see the world with new
eyes, to live our lives transformed in Christ and inspired
by the Spirit.

Living the resurrection

Some people understand 'living the resurrection' to mean
that we should be constantly (and, in my view, irritat-
ingly) cheerful, whatever the ups and downs of life. This
is far from the experience of the New Testament writers
who spoke often of real sufferings as a result of their life
in Christ. What it really means is that we enter the hard
times with our feet firmly planted on the rock, our souls
anchored in the hope that Christ brings. This does not
mean a lack of suffering or even that we do not feel suffering as much as others. It is one of many paradoxes
within the Christian tradition, which states that alongside
utter desolation lies glory, alongside agony, resurrection.
It does not lessen the pain but it can help us to trudge
on. It is a truth that sometimes we may cling to with the
very tips of our fingers, and in really bad times that we

lose touch of altogether, but it remains there waiting for us when we are able to embrace it once more. To believe in resurrection is to believe that death is not all powerful, that beyond despair there is hope or, as Paul puts it, that whatever life throws at us 'neither death, nor life, nor angels, nor rulers, nor things present, nor things to come, nor powers, nor height, nor depth, nor anything else in all creation, will be able to separate us from the love of God in Christ Jesus our Lord' (Romans 8.38–9).

This does not mean, however, that we will always feel this truth deep down. Faith is at least partially about keeping going despite what we feel today, tomorrow or the day after. Living the resurrection life includes expecting the sudden, powerful presence of the risen Jesus in the midst of our uncertainty and loss but trudging on whether we feel this presence or not. One of the most powerful witnesses to this has been the discovery, since her death, that Mother Teresa, to whom many people have looked over the years for inspiration in their own Christian journeys, did not, for much of her life, feel the presence of Jesus, and yet she kept going. Living the resurrection life does not imply we feel the resurrection life in us all the time but that we cling to it whatever life throws at us and seek to live out the principles of life beyond death, hope beyond despair and joy beyond sorrow in our everyday lives.

R. S. Thomas's poem 'Suddenly' (cited in full at the start of this chapter) encapsulates for me much of our relationship with the risen Christ. His expected, though always unexpected, presence appears silently and without fanfare, and then is gone almost before we have noticed it, suffusing our senses with the enormity of his being. One of the most tantalizing phrases of the whole poem comes at the end, when Thomas reflects that the robe for which the gamblers play is already worn by Jesus 'in this risen existence'. Which risen existence? His or ours? Of course, the answer, in the logic of the poem, is his but there is the merest hint that his risen existence somehow also becomes our own. The apostle Paul certainly thought so. This risen existence made possible through Christ's resurrection is now our own risen existence. At the start of this chapter I recalled how, as a child, I always felt there was more to resurrection than that Jesus is risen from the dead. I now know what that something more was and is. It is that it is not just Jesus who lives a risen existence but that I do too, as R. S. Thomas puts it, 'the whole of my being, overflowing with him as a chalice would with the sea'.

For further reading

Martha. Himmelfarb, *Ascent to Heaven in Jewish and Christian Apocalypses*, Oxford University Press, 1993.

Alan F. Segal, *Life After Death: A History of the Afterlife in Western Religion*, Doubleday Books, 2004.

Desmond Tutu, *No Future without Forgiveness,* Rider and Co., 1999.

Geza Vermes, *The Resurrection*, Penguin Books, 2008.

Rowan Williams, *Resurrection: Interpreting the Easter Gospel*, 2nd ed, Darton, Longman & Todd, 2002.

J. Edward Wright, *The Early History of Heaven*, Oxford University Press, 2002.

N. T. Wright, *Resurrection*, DVD, IVP Connect, 2006.

N. T. Wright, *The Resurrection of the Son of God*, SPCK, 2003.

I

LOOSE ENDS

The Resurrection in Mark's Gospel

Introduction

What do you consider a good ending to be? My children always ask me, when we start watching a film, whether it has a happy ending. If I say it doesn't, they refuse even to begin, and I must say I have a certain sympathy for them. I find it phenomenally hard to watch a film or read a book that doesn't promise a satisfyingly good ending (whether that be a happy one or simply one that ties together well the loose ends of the story). Mark's ending cannot by any stretch of anyone's imagination be called a 'good' ending. The narrative just peters out. It feels almost as though the author has run out of words and simply given up: the women ran away because they were afraid . . . In fact the existing ending seems so odd that later Christian tradition has supplied additional endings to make up for it. There is a shorter one (not given any verse numbers), a longer one (16.9–20) and endless supposition about lost endings and what they might have looked like.

Given my liking for a good ending, it is perhaps somewhat odd that I find this somewhat truncated ending to be entirely satisfying. There are many reasons for this, but the most important is that, in my view, the good news of Mark has not yet ended. Mark's Gospel is simply the prologue to the 'good news of Jesus Christ, son of God' (Mark 1.1), the story rolls on, borne out in the lives of each of us. The ending of the good news of Jesus Christ will not come for quite sometime yet; whether it is a good ending or not depends on us as much as on Mark.

❧

And the curtain of the temple was torn in two, from top to bottom. Now when the centurion, who stood facing him, saw that in this way he breathed his last, he said, 'Truly this man was God's Son!'

Mark 15.38–9

For further reading: Mark 15.27–47

Before you think that I have lost the plot, I know that this verse comes from the account of the crucifixion and is not a part of Mark's resurrection narrative, and yet, as with a number of the Gospel accounts of Jesus' death, it begins to give us a hint of what is to come. Up until this moment, the story of Jesus' death has been unremittingly bleak: his disciples have all run away, he has been scourged and mocked, soldiers have gambled for his clothing and now Jesus has died, abandoned and alone.

At this moment, however, a glimmer of light appears. Imagine a beam of sunshine breaking through heavy, black clouds on a stormy day. The clouds are still heavy, the atmosphere is still oppressive, the weather is still stormy but the beam of sunshine intimates that there may be more going on than we can see, and that above the clouds the sun shines. In the same way here, on one level nothing changes. Jesus is still dead – abandoned and alone – but then the most unlikely of people makes the pronouncement that Jesus 'was the (or a) Son of God' (Mark 15.38–9) and we also discover that he wasn't entirely alone. Far off in the distance stood some women, who had followed him during his ministry, and had followed him even here – albeit at a distance (Mark 15.40–1).

In Mark's gospel there are three moments where Jesus is declared to be God's son. At his baptism (Mark 1.9–11) when Jesus came up out of the water, he saw the heavens opened and heard God's voice proclaiming him to be the beloved Son of God; very similarly, at the transfiguration the three disciples who accompanied Jesus saw a cloud and heard a voice declaring him to be God's beloved son. The opening of heaven and the appearance of a cloud were both signs that this was a moment of divine revelation (see Acts 7.55 or Exodus 13.21 for other examples of these). Here the veil in the temple, which separates the Holy of Holies – the part of the temple where God dwelt in the midst of the people – from the rest of the temple, was ripped apart and we receive another revelation. This time, however, it is not God who speaks but a despised Roman centurion, one responsible for overseeing Jesus' death, who proclaims divine sonship for the Jesus who suffered and was crucified. Whether the centurion said that Jesus was *a* son of God or *the* Son of God (either is a possible translation of the Greek, as various scholars have pointed out), he recognized more in Jesus than the disciples had ever noticed during his life. His statement hangs before us as a challenge – whatever the centurion recognized in Jesus, whether it be that he was a special man or the Son of God – Who do you say that he was?

At this moment, even while Jesus hangs on the cross, a corner is turned. We travel with Jesus down to the very pits of despair, but then, when all seems lost, a beam of sunshine gleams, temporarily, through the gloom suggesting that this is, perhaps, not all there is to see: the despair is no less acute, the hopelessness still hangs in the air but perhaps, just perhaps, there is more. It is this sense of something beyond the hopelessness that is, for me, a vital part of our faith. It doesn't necessarily make the despair any less bleak, but it does give us a reason for trudging on.

ᘡᔕᕫᕐᕐᕂᕚ

But he said to them, 'Do not be alarmed; you are looking for Jesus of Nazareth, who was crucified. He has been raised; he is not here. Look, there is the place they laid him. But go, tell his disciples and Peter that he is going ahead of you to Galilee; there you will see him, just as he told you.'

Mark 16.6–7

For further reading: Mark 16.1–7

One of the things that most irritates me when I am upset is someone saying to me: 'Don't be upset.' This has to be one of the least helpful things that anyone can say and brings to mind that song, 'It's my party and I'll cry if I want to', or as the case may be 'it's my life and I'll be upset if I want to'. The only value of someone saying this to me, is that I get so irritated that I forget, at least for a while, why I was upset in the first place.

It strikes me that the angel's command to the women not to 'be alarmed' falls into this particular category of sayings. The Greek word has the resonance of being so utterly amazed that you actually feel disturbed or alarmed.

I rather think that this is entirely the appropriate response to turning up at a tomb in order to grieve for a loved one who has died in the most gruesome of circumstances, only to find the tomb empty of everything but an angel. In fact, my emotions would be a lot stronger than amazed to the point of alarm. Why then does the angel tell the women not to be alarmed? I suspect that this is due to the second command that the angel gives the women, that they should 'go, tell' Peter and the disciples that Jesus has risen from the dead. If the women spent too long in a state of amazement and alarm the all-important message would remain unproclaimed, unannounced to those who needed to hear it most. As it happens, it is very clear in Mark's Gospel that the angel's command had as little effect on the women as the command not to be upset has on me: they remained alarmed, in fact their emotion seems to become stronger. Verse 8 tells us that they fled in terror – now not just alarmed but frightened out of their minds.

This command to 'go, tell' is hugely important in Mark, because before this moment the disciples and those who were healed were told time and time again not to tell anyone anything. Jesus' command to keep quiet, it seems, was not a permanent one but a temporary one, they were to wait until they had the best news of all to proclaim before they told what they knew about Jesus. In fact, Jesus even made this explicit at one point in his ministry when he said that Peter, James and John were not to mention the transfiguration to anyone until Jesus had risen from the dead (Mark 9.9). The reason for this was probably because they would have got the wrong end of the stick, as the disciples so often did. For example, in Caeserea Philippi, when Jesus asked Peter who he thought Jesus was, Peter responded 'You are the Christ', but then went on to rebuke Jesus when Jesus declared that he must therefore suffer and die. Peter's understanding of who Jesus was, was at best partial. If he had gone out proclaiming Jesus too early then he would have made Jesus into someone that he wasn't.

They were now in full control of all the facts. They had seen Jesus' ministry, heard his teaching, seen him relate to the poor and outcasts, seen him die and now knew that he had risen from the dead. Now was the time to put the pieces together and to go and proclaim it – and somewhat inevitably, the women ran terrified from the tomb. What they now knew of Jesus was almost too much to grasp. If I had been there, I suspect that whatever the angel said, I would have run away even faster than they did.

༁ఌఌ

So they went out and fled from the tomb, for terror and amazement had seized them; and they said nothing to anyone, for they were afraid.

Mark 16.8

I've always been intrigued by the philosophical riddle, 'If a tree falls in a forest and no one is around to hear it, does it make a sound?' because the instinctual reaction is: of course it does. A sound is a sound whether we hear it or not. Isn't it? Apparently the scientific explanation is no it isn't, since sound is the vibration transmitted to our senses via the ear. If no ear is there to receive the vibration then no sound is made.

The ending to Mark's Gospel begs a similar question. If Jesus was risen from the dead and no one said anything about it, would that undermine the power of his rising from the dead? Of course, we – the readers of Mark

– know that this is an entirely hypothetical question. The fact that we are reading that the women ran away and said nothing, tells us that at some point they did say something to someone; otherwise we would know nothing at all of what happened at the tomb.

Nevertheless, the question remains. If the women had never said anything to anyone, would the power of the resurrection be undermined? Hardly surprisingly, there is a yes and no answer to give here. Yes, it would reduce the power of the resurrection because God in his great and unfathomable generosity has seen fit to trust us to communicate the things of God in the world. If we choose not to then of course this will detract from the wonder of the event. This is something that lies particularly heavily on the mind of Paul the apostle who in Romans 10.14 asks how people will believe if they have not heard. For Paul there is an appropriate urgency and importance about sharing the good news of Jesus' death and subsequent rising from the dead.

On the other hand, however, it is important to recognize that even if the women had said nothing, ever, to anyone, Jesus would still be risen, the resurrection would still have happened, death and sin would still be defeated. Even if the women had said nothing, the disciples would have learnt of Jesus' resurrection when he appeared to them in Galilee; even if we decide never to take up the challenge to 'go, tell', God will still be God and Jesus will still be risen. God invites our engagement in his divine plan but does not need it. Failure of nerve on the part of human beings does not ruin God's presence in the world.

I am reminded here of a passage from Steff Penney's wonderful novel, *The Tenderness of Wolves*, in which one of the characters speaks of her time in a mental hospital where she had met a man who believed that he had been spoken to by God and told to invent a steam engine that would save the world from sin. This became his life's obsession and what tormented him most was the knowledge of his own significance: if he did not complete the engine the world would come to nothing. The character says: 'He knew how important he was in the scheme of things, and would seize each of us in the grounds and beg us to help him escape, so he could continue his vital work. Among those tortured souls, almost all of them bewailing some private anguish, his beseeching were the most heartbreaking I ever heard . . . such is the torment of knowing your own significance.' It is very easy to fall into the trap of believing in our own significance. In my view, the ending of Mark's Gospel puts everything beautifully into perspective. We are invited to join in with the proclamation of some of the best news possible – that Jesus is risen from the dead – but even if, like the women at the tomb, we are overcome with terror and run away, Jesus will still be risen. God has made us far more significant in his divine plan than we deserve to be but not so significant that we should ever be in danger of losing our sanity because it all depends on us.

Concluding reflections

The oldest manuscripts of Mark end with 16.8 and, as I said above, for me this works as an ending. Some people point out that if we end with verse 8 then the Greek text finishes with the word 'for', since the Greek literally says, 'They ran away. They were afraid for.' To people schooled in good English grammar this is a terrible ending: you may have had drummed into you, as I did, that you should *never* end a sentence with words like and, but or for. This may be a rule of English grammar, but it is not a rule of Greek grammar, where the word 'for', must always come second in a sentence. If you should want to have a two word sentence that includes the word 'for' the only place for it to go is at the end.

The ending of Mark's Gospel fits the rest of the Gospel. It ends on a knife edge: will the disciples finally realize who Jesus is and live up to the high calling to which he attempted to point them throughout his life? Or will they, as so often before, fail him, running away at the key moment when they are most needed? The answer seems to be yes to both questions: yes they do fail him again but the fact that we are now reading the Gospel, written probably about 40 years after these events, tells us that ultimately they did not fail and did live up to Jesus' expectations of them. We so often want to make a clear-cut decision on whether the disciples were good or bad, successes or failures. The answer seems to be that they were a mix of both good and bad, successful and failing and this should surely be very comforting to all of us who struggle along the way of discipleship today.

2

DRAMATIC EVENTS

The Resurrection in Matthew's Gospel

Introduction

If your liking is for a story that is dramatic – almost melodramatic – with plenty of action, then Matthew's Gospel is the one for you. It is Matthew's Gospel that describes rocks splitting at Jesus' death, which allowed many of the 'holy ones' to rise from the dead and roam around Jerusalem. It also describes an earthquake at the resurrection, the guards falling over in a trance, and a commission that sent the disciples to proclaim the gospel to the whole world. Matthew's account of Jesus' death and resurrection would not be out of place in a modern science fiction film.

Where John's Gospel tells us about the resurrection from the perspective of the personal relationships between Jesus and Mary, Thomas and Peter, Matthew recounts a broader, wider picture, which tells of the way in which the resurrection made a difference to the world as a whole – even to the point of causing an earthquake. Where Mark's Gospel leaves us unsure about whether anyone will ever discover that the resurrection has happened, here the resurrection rocks the whole world, demanding attention and response.

❧

At that moment the curtain of the temple was torn in two, from top to bottom. The earth shook, and the rocks were split. The tombs also were opened, and many bodies of the saints who had fallen asleep were raised. After his resurrection they came out of the tombs and entered the holy city and appeared to many.

Matthew 27.51–3

I am a remarkably unobservant witness. On the few occasions when I've been asked to act as a witness to something that has happened I've been near useless: 'It was two men, or maybe three; they were quite tall – but then to me most men seem tall – one had a black, no blue hoodie or maybe jacket on.' I normally end up feeling sorry for the poor police having to take the statement down who have to cross out what they have written so often that it is a mass of black – or was that blue – ink.

Matthew's account of Jesus' death and resurrection leaves no doubt about the importance of what has happened (even for someone as unobservant as I am): the ripping of curtains, the shaking of earth, the splitting of tombs and the resurrection of some of the dead is enough drama to catch even my absent-minded attention.

Matthew wants to make sure that we understand the significance of Jesus' death. Everything that takes place is there to reinforce the message that this is a moment of revelation (as we saw in Mark's Gospel) but also that something in the world has shifted irrevocably. Tombs are split open ready for a resurrection of the holy ones to take place, when Jesus himself rises from the dead. This is a detail that reinforces as clearly as it can that Jesus' death is about to change the world significantly, the end times are about to begin – though not completely, for that we must wait until the end of all times. Jesus' death marked the brink between the old and the new, the world now waited poised for the resurrection to take place and for glimmers of the end times to be found in the world.

The shaking of the earth, the splitting of the rocks and the breaking open of the tombs are all features that would have persuaded Matthew's audience that what had happened was a moment of divine revelation. Though the irony is, that the very thing that Matthew knew his readers needed to convince them of the importance of what had happened, is precisely what makes it hardest for us – a modern audience – to believe. Most people can just about cope with the splitting of the curtain in the temple, darkness falling over the whole land, and Jesus' resurrection, but add in an additional earthquake, rocks exploding and a more general resurrection of the dead and we really begin to struggle.

There is no easy solution to the problem. Questioning the historicity of the Matthean account is a little like pulling on a thread at the top of your jumper; you may get rid of that annoying loose end but then discover that you've unravelled the whole lot and find yourself left with just a tangled heap of wool. On the other hand, insisting implacably that Matthew must be believed in every last detail, feels, for some people at least, too much like swallowing camels. So what are we to do? My own solution is to ask what Matthew was trying to tell us by including these details. In other words, what did he want his audience to believe about Jesus and the world once they had read this passage? This is quite clear. For Matthew Jesus' death was the signal that the world now stood on the brink of something entirely new; God has already begun to intervene in the world. For me, asking these kind of questions avoids us getting caught down the cul-de-sac of historical questions which, though important, often lead us to miss the whole point of what the New Testament is talking about. This is a solution that works for me, but I do recognize that it won't work for everyone.

✿

And suddenly there was a great earthquake; for an angel of the Lord, descending from heaven, came and rolled back the stone and sat on it. His appearance was like lightning, and his clothing white as snow. For fear of him the guards shook and became like dead men.

Matthew 28.2–4

For further reading: Matthew 28.1–8

My family really enjoy corny jokes, like 'What begins with a "c" and sound like a parrot? – a carrot or 'What looks like an elephant and flies?' – a flying elephant. What makes these jokes funny – or at any rate mildly amusing – is that they state the obvious. We, particularly as adults, try to think of fancy and complex answers and most of the time we are caught out by missing the blindingly obvious answer right under our noses.

Matthew's account of the resurrection asks one of those blindingly obvious questions (though not here in the form of a joke). If you feel an earthquake, see a being whose appearance is like lightning and whose clothing is as white as snow, who is it? Our problem, of course, is that we have no idea. Matthew was speaking to an audience many of whom would have known immediately what and who he was talking about. We, however, are slightly bemused. Matthew has told us it is an angel so we accept what he says but do not really know why.

Matthew gives a whole tool kit of clues about what he is talking about, which someone well versed in Old Testament imagery could spot. The first clue is the earthquake. Throughout the Old Testament, the presence of God was signalled by natural phenomena such as wind, lightning, thunder, hail, fire and earthquakes. For someone who saw the world through first century Hebrew eyes, the mention of an earthquake might immediately suggest divine presence. The appearance of the angel is also significant. There are suggestions of Jesus' transfiguration, because at the transfiguration Jesus wore a white garment (see Matthew 17.2), but there are also links to the book of Daniel where God is described as having clothing that was 'as white as snow' (Daniel 7.9–10) and the the man who appeared to Daniel had a face 'like lightning' (Daniel 12.6).

Matthew's audience would have known that this was a being who had come directly from the presence of God. In this context, the response of the guards was appropriate: being even this close to God's presence was highly dangerous. The Hebrew tradition, which stated that people who saw the face of God could die, was one that was still current at the time of Jesus and, in fact, became even stronger in the centuries immediately following Jesus. In the light of this tradition, such strong hints of divine presence would have been terrifying for anyone who was present. The only sensible response was fear, something that was underlined by the words of the angel to the women; although the wording is lost in most English translations, the angel said to the women 'You, do not be afraid', that is, they, the guards, do well to fear but you should not. This is because straying inadvertently into God's presence was dangerous, but being there because you were invited to be, as the women were, was not. Just like Moses, Elijah and Isaiah before them, the women survived their experience of being in God's presence because they were invited into that presence before being sent onwards to proclaim God's message as he commanded them to.

The irony of the guards' response, though, was that this was a place in which Jesus, who was dead, had now come alive; the guards, who were alive, became as though they were dead. In the face of overwhelming, transformative life, the guards became like corpses (the Greek word is the word used simply for a lifeless, breathless body). I can't help wondering whether their response is, sadly, typical of our own responses to the news of the vibrant, risen, transforming Christ. Overcome by fear, do we become lifeless and unresponsive to the whirling, challenging, inspiring presence of the risen Christ? Or can we allow ourselves to be open to the transforming – albeit unsafe – demands of the God who brings the dead to life?

❧

Now the eleven disciples went to Galilee, to the mountain to which Jesus had directed them. When they saw him, they worshiped him; but some doubted.

Matthew 28.16–17

For further reading: Matthew 28.9–17

The word 'doubt' is one of those much-abused words in our English language. We all have our most hated phrases of words or phrases that are over-used and have changed their meaning. A recent *Daily Telegraph* poll put the use of the word 'literally' at the top of their most hated words or phrases, whereas another poll put 'at the end of the day' and 'fairly unique' at the top. One of my most hated phrases is 'with respect', a phrase that almost invariably will be followed by something not at all respectful. I think we often use the word 'doubt' in a similar way – 'I very much doubt that' often means 'I am confident you are wrong', and 'I have my doubts' can mean 'I am about to tell you why you are wrong.' The word doubt, however, means nothing like this. It is the word that stands precisely between belief and unbelief; it is not weighted more to unbelief than to belief. It simply marks a lack of sureness.

When you think about what the disciples needed to assimilate, it is hardly surprising that some of them doubted. They have seen their beloved and trusted leader die a gruesome and distressing death, the women at the tomb have seen an earthquake, an angel wearing divine garments and, in verse 9, Jesus himself risen from the dead. The authorities have been putting around a story that Jesus' body has been stolen and now, on a mountain in Galilee they see the risen Jesus face to face. I would say that in these circumstances doubting is a good option – not disbelieving but keeping a mind open, unclosed, working on it until clarity arises.

We live in a world obsessed by certainty. We are meant to hold clear, confident views on subjects that range widely from education to euthanasia, from economics to the environment – and to express our clear, certain views regularly in on-line polls and surveys and in conversation. This is something that irritates me almost as much as the phrase 'with respect'. In my view, premature certainty is as corrosive of truth as lies can be. Certain things in life need time for reflection as we wrestle with issues, questions and explore possibilities. Rushing too swiftly to an immovable certainty undermines our ability to grasp the truth.

One of my favourite features of this Matthean story is

that, when they encountered the risen Christ, the disciples worshipped but some of them doubted. It wasn't just the non-doubters who worshipped but, the story implies, all of them. This is not the only place in Matthew's Gospel where doubt and worship intertwine. We find it also in Matthew 14.25–36, where Peter tries to walk on the water like Jesus and begins to sink. After he got into the boat Jesus asked Peter why he doubted and those in the boat, including the doubting Peter, worshipped him. Today we often feel that we can only worship if we are clear in our views, if we have dotted all the 'i's and crossed all the 't's. Doubt can be seen to be the antithesis of worship. It is not. We worship not out of our certainty but out of our response to God. Fortunately, we do not have to comprehend everything about God and God's relationship with the world before we worship. In fact, sometimes it is our doubts that can draw us deeper into the mystery of God, and from deep within the mystery of God the only possible thing to do is worship.

❧

And Jesus came and said to them, 'All authority in heaven and on earth has been given to me. Go therefore and make disciples of all nations, baptizing them in the name of the Father and of the Son and of the Holy Spirit, and teaching them to obey everything that I have commanded you. And remember, I am with you always, to the end of the age.'

Matthew 28.18–20

I remember once being taught how to make an origami crane (the bird variety not the mechanical kind). The person teaching me showed me once, and then again, then a third time and finally in response to my blank look sent me off to show someone else how to do it. I would like to tell you that the resulting crane was pristine, well creased in the right places (and not in the wrong places) and recognizably what it was meant to be; I would like to tell you that but, of course, I would be lying. Nevertheless, the bird was my best effort so far and at least better than it would have been otherwise.

This passage from Matthew's Gospel, often called the 'Great Commission', feels a little risky. This is Matthew's Gospel, not Mark's, so the disciples aren't portrayed as quite such a liability as they are in Mark's narrative, Nevertheless, they have not yet demonstrated much ability to comprehend who Jesus really is let alone to make new disciples on his behalf. Only a few verses before, we are told that they worshipped Jesus but some doubted. These are no expert Jesus followers fully ready and primed for action. The Great Commission does seem to fall – at least slightly – into the same category as my would-be origami teacher's instructions to me, of sending them off before they had completely understood everything in order to help them to complete the learning process for themselves.

It also provides us with a challenge. It is tempting to use our lack of readiness as an excuse to duck out of this commission: 'I don't feel fully prepared yet. Maybe one more course, a little more learning, another year's reflection and then maybe I will be ready.' One of the striking features of Jesus in his ministry is his – to our mind – almost irresponsible and certainly risky willingness to send us out just as we are to carry on the task he began among the disciples, before we feel anything like ready. In the midst of our fragile, half-glimpsed understandings of God, in the midst of our doubting and uncertainty Jesus still calls us to be to others as he was to the earliest disciples. We don't have to be ready, but we do have to do it.

It isn't as daunting as it may seem. Jesus made disciples simply by calling them and then by being with them. The earliest disciples lived alongside Jesus, asked questions, got things wrong, asked more questions, watched him, got things wrong again, asked questions again. All this, as they carried on their daily lives, ate together and travelled together. The making of disciples culminates in baptizing and teaching what Jesus has taught but it begins in our everyday life; in our relationships, our meals together, the common ordinariness of life. It is here that discipleship begins and here that Jesus commands us to draw others to him just as he commanded the earliest disciples. In doing so we will discover that we are not just making disciples of others but that we are transforming our own discipleship into something deeper and more Christ-like than it was before.

Concluding reflections

Matthew's account of Jesus' death and resurrection is somewhat different from Mark's. Mark's Gospel leaves us with untied ends and unfinished business. At the end of Mark we are left to work out quite a lot for ourselves about how we might respond to the Jesus who is now risen from the dead. In contrast, Matthew's Gospel is entirely clear. Supernatural events like the dead rising from their tombs, earthquakes and rocks splitting apart leave us in no doubt about the significance of what has happened and Jesus himself tells the disciples what they must now do. The effect, however, is similar. Both Mark and Matthew leave us with a clear expectation that Jesus' resurrection will spur us on to tell others about it. This is good news far, far too good to keep to ourselves.

3

ON THE WAY

The Resurrection in Luke's Gospel

Introduction

Each one of the Gospels (with the exception of Mark, which we have already noted is unusual in a number of ways) tells of two major resurrection appearances: one immediately after the resurrection, normally around the tomb, and the other somewhere else, in which Jesus commissions the disciples to further action. In Matthew Jesus first meets the women as they run from the tomb and then all the disciples as a group on the mountain where he gives them the great commission. In John, Jesus meets Mary near the tomb and then the disciples in a locked room where he breathes the Spirit on them (John's Gospel also has two additional appearances: one to Thomas and one by the lake, where Peter is commissioned personally).

Luke's Gospel follows this rough pattern but in an unusual way. Jesus' first appearance occurs not near the tomb but on the way to Emmaus. Peter runs to the tomb and looks in but sees nothing except empty grave clothes. It is only in the iconic story of the two disciples travelling to Emmaus that Jesus appears for the first time. His resurrection is revealed, then, as with so many other events in Luke's Gospel in a journey, on the way.

༨ᢀ

He replied, 'Truly I tell you, today you will be with me in Paradise.'

Luke 23.43

For further reading: Luke 23.39–43

The word 'Paradise' has passed into common language and we find it all over the place. There is, I discover, a webmail site, a cruise ship, countless holiday resorts, a wildlife park and even a town in Nevada all called Paradise. Calling these things paradise is intended to evoke peace, tranquillity and general well-being and hence to make us want to seek it out, but what did the criminal on the cross understand Jesus to mean when he promised that he, the criminal, would be with Jesus in paradise today? Although we know that it was unlikely that he expected a beach holiday with miles of golden sands or even a cruise, it is harder to work out what he *was* expecting.

The word 'paradise' comes from a Greek word, which in its turn probably came from a Persian word that meant an enclosed park or garden (that is, one with a wall around it). It is used a number of times in the Greek version of the Old Testament to refer either to gardens in general or to the very specific Garden of Eden, which was closed and sealed after Adam and Eve were driven out in Genesis 3. As time went by, different beliefs grew up about whether Paradise was on earth or in heaven. Some thought that it was still on earth but hidden, others that it had been taken up into heaven. Thus, although we now use the word almost interchangeably with the word 'heaven', in Jewish use it was not exactly the same: paradise, if in heaven, was a place (the Garden of Eden) within heaven. What is important, however, is that paradise/Garden of Eden was thought to have been sealed when Adam and Eve left it and to remain sealed until the last days, when it would be open to humanity once more.

One of the reasons for this was that it contains the tree of life (the tree that allows people to live forever). Since humanity was declared by God to be mortal, the fruit of this tree cannot be tasted until the end of time; an interesting reference to this can be found in the book of Revelation 2.7 ('to everyone who conquers, I will give permission to eat from the tree of life that is in the paradise of God'). In those last days, the righteous would be able to regain what had been lost to Adam and Eve; the garden of Eden would be open again and God could once more walk among us in the cool of the evening.* If the criminal is to be with Jesus in paradise *today* then the garden of Eden has been re-opened and Jesus' death on the cross has enabled that re-opening to take place now.

What this brief exploration of paradise tells us is that Jesus' words from the cross had far, far more significance than we usually give them. The invitation to the criminal to be with Jesus in paradise *today* tells us that at Jesus' death paradise is being re-opened and that the end of time has already begun. From now on the world will be a different place. This is not just a promise of forgiveness and hope to one dying criminal but to the whole world, a world that can now live in the knowledge of paradise reopened and humanity reunited with God. Each one of the Gospels contains within the narrative of the crucifixion a glimmer of the resurrection: this is Luke's glimmer

---

* For anyone who is interested, the only exception to this within the Bible is the person in Christ's reported visit to Paradise (2 Corinthians 12.4) which is clearly only temporary – the person in Christ (who in my view was Paul) visited Paradise and then left again.

of resurrection. A glimmer that speaks powerfully of a world transformed and renewed.

❧

Now it was Mary Magdalene, Joanna, Mary the mother of James, and the other women with them who told this to the apostles. But these words seemed to them an idle tale, and they did not believe them. But Peter got up and ran to the tomb; stooping and looking in, he saw the linen cloths by themselves; then he went home, amazed at what had happened.

Luke 24.10–12

For further reading: Luke 24.1–12

Whenever I go to the hairdressers, I find myself entertained by my attitude to glossy magazines, which are run on gossip such as who has split up with whom, which glamorous couples were seen out together or should have been seen out together and weren't. A large portion of me thinks that these magazines are a complete waste of time and not worth reading at all, and yet another part of me loves them. On arriving at the hairdressers I sit for a while pretending that I would never read magazines like that and slowly I crumble. I pick one up, flick through it idly and then end up engrossed in a story that some, using Luke's words, might call an 'idle tale'. The content of these magazines, while riveting to some extent, is not of any great significance.

It is almost inconceivable, to me, that the women's account to the disciples of an empty tomb, angelic visitors and Jesus' resurrection from the dead can be put in the similar category of 'idle tales'. This passing phrase in Luke ('the words seemed to them like an idle tale') communicates a maelstrom of emotion. We can read between these lines deep tensions caused by the dismissal of the women in a rather superior way by the eleven and frustration by the women for being written off, especially at the point when what they had to say was so very important. Only Peter decided to see for himself and, running to the tomb, found enough corroborating evidence for him to be amazed.

This seemingly unimportant phrase reminds us that we write off people and what they say at our peril. No doubt the disciples felt that they were perfectly right to ignore what the women said, as we so often do when we depreciate things. The problem is that while our instincts are often right, they are sometimes wrong. In this instance, what seemed like an idle tale was, in fact, the most important news that they were ever likely to receive. When they wrote off the women's tale, they placed themselves in great danger of missing this good news altogether. We do not know why the eleven dismissed the women's tale. It could have been simply because they were women; it could have been because these particular women had a penchant for gossip that the eleven had learnt to distrust; it could have been because the eleven were simply not ready to hear the good news no matter who brought it.

Often Peter is held up as a 'big-footed' fool: too quick to open his mouth, unable to comprehend what it means for Jesus to be the Messiah and, most catastrophically of all, denying Jesus when he needed him most. Here, however, he demonstrated a vital characteristic of what true discipleship is – going to see for yourself. He neither trusted too quickly nor disbelieved too quickly but went to have a look so that he could make up his own mind. If anything, Peter's action here represents true discipleship: listening, thinking, exploring and coming to your own conclusion. So often we confuse what Jesus called the disciples to do (follow him) with what a disciple really is (someone who learns). The essence of discipleship is learning. As disciples of Jesus we learn best by following him and being with him, but following by itself does not make us disciples. It seems that Peter has, at last, become the learner that Jesus yearned for him to be: willing to listen, to explore and to work things out for himself. This is what discipleship is and it is what we are still called to today.

✃ ❧

Now on that same day two of them were going to a village called Emmaus, about seven miles from Jerusalem, and talking with each other about all these things that had happened. While they were talking and discussing, Jesus himself came near and went with them, but their eyes were kept from recognizing him. And he said to them, 'What are you discussing with each other while you walk along?' They stood still, looking sad.

Luke 24.13–17

For further reading: Luke 24.13–27

Have you ever been caught in the middle of someone else's argument and not known quite what to do? Intervene? Walk away? Change the subject? Let it run its course? Jesus, it appears, had no such problems. The well-loved story of the meeting on the road to Emmaus tells of two disciples who, on the day of Jesus' resurrection, decided to return home to a little-known village – Emmaus. As they went they were deep in discussion, or possibly were having a full-blown row. The words that Luke uses to describe what they are doing increase with intensity. When we first encounter them Luke tells us that they are 'conversing' (the word translated 'talking' in verse 14 and again in 15). When Luke uses 'conversing' for a second time he adds another word 'disputing' or 'debating'. The heat is a little higher and the conversation more fervent. However, when Jesus asked them about it in verse 17 (translated in the NRSV as 'What are you discussing with each other while you walk along?') an entirely different word (*antiballo*) is used, which comes from the Greek word for 'throw' and was used in Greek literature to describe people throwing things at each other or at a target in the gymnasium or games.

The implication, then, is that Jesus has come across these two in the middle of a discussion that has developed into a full-blown argument. As so often in Luke, we are left to use our imaginations to fill in the gaps. What were they arguing about? Why were they leaving Jerusalem at all if they had heard the account of Jesus' resurrection? Who were they? We do not know, but I cannot help wondering whether the few clues that Luke does give us suggest that this is a married couple in the midst of a marital argument (apart from anything else it is worth remembering that these two lived in the same house in Emmaus). One of the disciples is named Cleopas, an abbreviation of the longer name Cleopatros, and may also be the Greek version of the Hebrew name Clopas. This is important because we know of a Clopas from John's Gospel, where one of the women standing near the cross is revealed to be Mary wife of Clopas. If for a moment we allow ourselves a flight of fancy, it is just possible that the two that Jesus meets are Clopas and Mary, arguing about what has happened and about why they are leaving Jerusalem right at that moment.

As so often, Luke provides us with just the bare bones of the story because the identity of the two on the road is not the main point. The main point is that when Jesus asked them in verse 17 what they were arguing about they stood gloomily (the Greek word communicates a certain sullenness) but when they returned to Jerusalem at the end of the story they ran back as fast as their legs would take them, talking about how their hearts burned within them. The risen Christ stepped into the heart of their argument, transforming them from being sullen and worn down by their disappointment, into people filled with energy and enthusiasm. This is the kind of conflict resolution that all our communities – both local and global – so desperately need, a resolution that, in the person of Christ, meets us on the way, breaks into our arguments and transforms our sullen misery to joyful enthusiasm.

But they urged him strongly, saying, 'Stay with us, because it is almost evening and the day is now nearly over.' So he went in to stay with them. When he was at the table with them, he took bread, blessed and broke it, and gave it to them. Then their eyes were opened, and they recognized him; and he vanished from their sight. They said to each other, 'Were not our hearts burning within us while he was talking to us on the road, while he was opening the scriptures to us?'

Luke 24.29–32

For further reading: Luke 24.27–32

One of the greatest pleasures in life can be sharing a meal with someone. Over shared food we can relax, feel more at ease and share more of ourselves than we might in other situations. Hospitality is widely regarded around the world as an essential part of relationship. In western culture the word 'hospitality' has the suggestion of entertaining friends (in a social setting) or clients (in a business setting). For us, hospitality implies some kind of prior connection with those to whom we offer it. The origin of the word is somewhat different. The word 'hospitality' has as one of its roots the Latin word '*hospes*' which is related to the word for stranger and this is what ancient hospitality was all about. The act of welcoming a stranger into the home, caring for them, protecting them and sending them on their way lies at the heart of many stories not only in the Bible but in Greek and Latin mythology as well.

Indeed, there grew up a widespread tradition that it was essential to welcome strangers because they might be angels in disguise (see, for example, Hebrews 13.2: 'Do not neglect to show hospitality to strangers, for by doing that some have entertained angels without knowing it'). The story of meeting Jesus on the road to Emmaus has points of overlap with this tradition, though in reverse. In most of the stories about welcoming angels, the stranger is welcomed and, once hospitality has been received, a revelation happens that tells the host something that they had not known previously. In this story all of this is turned on its head. The revelation takes place on the road, and before they even reach Emmaus Jesus explains the scriptures to them. When they reach their house, they urge Jesus to stay but once they sit to eat Jesus takes over as host (in Judaism it is the host, and only the host, who breaks and blesses bread). When the moment of recognition occurs it becomes as clear to the two disciples as it has always been to us, the readers, that the stranger on the way was in fact not a stranger at all, but their dearest friend.

All of this came together through hospitality. In the previous section, we noted how important it was that the two disciples were transformed through their encounter with Jesus on the way. We now discover that this transformation happened through hospitality. Often much is made of the fact that the disciples only recognized Jesus when he performed the action of breaking bread (something that he did with his followers over and over again during his lifetime). This is indeed a key to the story: it was in Jesus' action not just in his words that recognition took place. The action of the breaking of bread, however, only became possible because first the disciples had offered Jesus hospitality. As they travelled with Jesus to Emmaus Jesus offered to them the untold riches of his own interpretation of scripture but the disciples were only able to realize the significance of this when they reached out to offer Jesus food and shelter. Only when they sought to give to him, could they truly receive what he offered. It is the paradox of true hospitality that in giving we receive and in welcoming strangers we find friendship, and that in the meeting the needs of a stranger, Jesus meets with us.

While they were talking about this, Jesus himself stood among them and said to them, 'Peace be with you.' They were startled and terrified, and thought that they were seeing a ghost. He said to them, 'Why are you frightened, and why do doubts arise in your hearts?'

Luke 24.36-8

For further reading: Luke 24.34-53

Knowing something, and really knowing it so that we have processed all its implications are two entirely different things. I regularly discover this with the planning of our family diary. I know, for example, that I am in London all day; I also know that my husband is away at a meeting; I know again that one of my daughters needs to go to Brownies and the other one to have a friend to play but it often takes me a while to realize that this is going to cause problems! The first kind of knowing is simply a listing of facts, the second involves putting things together, joining up the dots and drawing conclusions. The two are important but do not necessarily flow on, one from another. We can know things without comprehending what they mean, as I have discovered to my cost.

It is easy to wonder why the disciples were so terrified when Jesus turned up in the room. They have just that very moment been discussing the double revelation of the resurrected Jesus to Simon and then to the two on the way to Emmaus. Why then are they terrified when he appears among them? And why do they assume that he is a ghost when they have just heard that he is risen? The answer almost certainly lies with this difference in knowledge. They know of Jesus' resurrection with their heads but have not yet let that knowledge seep into them so that they fully understand what it means, can comprehend the consequences and can live accordingly.

I wonder whether we, like the disciples, struggle to get our heads around the consequences of Jesus' resurrection. It is much easier to know *that* Jesus has risen from the dead and even to proclaim it, than it is to live in the light of its happening. All too often we become locked into pre-resurrection ways of viewing the world, of accepting that things are impossible, bleak and without hope. Living the resurrection involves seeing the world through different eyes: seeing life where there appears to be only death, possibility in the impossible, hope in despair and renewal in stagnation. On more than one occasion in his letters the apostle Paul talks about God as the one who raised Jesus from the dead. For him the resurrection was more than an event – it was a divine characteristic. If God is that kind of God then we must live expectant lives in which we look for and find evidence of resurrection in our everyday lives.

This is not a facile 'always looking on the bright side of life' but a much deeper seeing of the world through new eyes, expecting the God who can raise Jesus from the dead to transform our own stultifying, life-draining impossibilities into something new and life giving. All too often, however, we react like the earliest disciples. We know that Jesus is risen from the dead, we talk about it and sing about it and yet are terrified and amazed when he actually appears in our midst.

Concluding reflections

Luke's resurrection narratives seem to be about comprehending the fullness of what it means for Jesus to be risen from the dead, or as R. S. Thomas puts it in his poem 'Suddenly' (quoted at the start of the Introduction, p. XX): 'not with the eye only but with the whole of my being'. We begin, in Luke, with the fact of the resurrection – the tomb is empty, the grave clothes abandoned and it is announced that Jesus is alive. This fact is reported by the women, who are dismissed by the other disciples, and then Peter. The rest of the stories are about people being transformed by the reality of this fact when they experience Jesus for themselves: the two on the road to Emmaus become animated and full of energy, and the disciples who eat with him worship him.

It causes me great joy – and a certain amount of envy –

as a student of the Bible to discover that in both of Luke's resurrection accounts a major feature of Jesus' time with the disciples after the resurrection was the unfolding of the scriptures to the disciples, causing their hearts to burn on the way to Emmaus, and opening their minds on the mountain top. At the same time, it is important to recognize that it was not the biblical interpretation alone that transformed the disciples but their recognition of who Jesus was. Interpretation and experience go hand in hand. Their experience of the risen Jesus helps them to understand the profundity of the interpretation they have received, but the interpretation helps them to comprehend the significance of their experience. It is both of these together that caused the disciples to spend the whole of their time in the temple worshipping God, which is where Luke leaves them as the Gospel ends.

4

MY LORD AND MY GOD

The Resurrection in John's Gospel

Introduction

In many ways the Gospel of John is the resurrection Gospel. We have twice as many resurrection appearances in John as in the other Gospels. We have already noticed that the resurrection experiences are of two kinds. One, an initial experience, confirms the fact of Jesus' resurrection and helps the recipient(s) to comprehend what it means (as with the women in Matthew and the two on the road to Emmaus in Luke) and the other, a further experience normally to a bigger group, which also commissions the disciples to further action. Matthew and Luke have one of each of these types of resurrection experiences, whereas John has two of each. First, Mary sees Jesus in the garden, then Jesus sends the spirit on the disciples. Then we have another two: Thomas sees and comprehends Jesus, and then at the meal by the sea Jesus commissions Peter to care for his 'sheep'. John gives us twice the impact of the resurrection in two lots of two accounts.

For those of you who wonder why I've missed it out, I have put the first commissioning account (John 20.19–23) – in which Jesus sends his Spirit on the disciples – into the cluster of readings at the end of the book around Pentecost, rather than here with the resurrection. In many ways this is an artificial distinction. In John's Gospel the death, resurrection and ascension of Jesus, together with the sending of the Spirit, are so closely linked that it is hard to pull them apart. Nevertheless, it helps us to see how John treats the Spirit if we put this passage alongside the other Spirit passages later in the book.

❧

And just as Moses lifted up the serpent in the wilderness, so must the Son of Man be lifted up, that whoever believes in him may have eternal life. For God so loved the world that he gave his only Son, so that everyone who believes in him may not perish but may have eternal life. Indeed, God did not send the Son into the world to condemn the world, but in order that the world might be saved through him.

John 3.14–17

For further reading: John 3.1–21

At the west end of the Church of St James the Great, Shirley, in the Birmingham Diocese, there is a sculpture by Josefina de Vasconcellos which depicts Jesus. It is high up on the wall, and in the sculpture Jesus has his arms stretched out wide. What is not clear, however, is whether it depicts the crucifixion, the resurrection or the ascension. Are the arms held open on the cross or in love for the world? Is Jesus lifted high in mockery or in victory? Is Jesus held to the cross or ascending into heaven? One of the things I love about the sculpture is that it asks exactly the same questions that John's Gospel does. In Matthew,

Mark and Luke it is very clear that the crucifixion is the
moment of despair and the resurrection the moment of
victory and joy. In John's Gospel this distinction is much
less clear. In John, Jesus' death is a time of despair intermingled with joy, of heartache intermingled with victory.
It is almost as though in John's mind the death and resurrection spill into each other, so that they become almost,
though not quite, the same event.

This is made even clearer by the fact that, in John's
Gospel, when Jesus looks into the future to his death and
resurrection, he uses the phrase 'lifted up', as in John 3.14
('so must the Son of Man be lifted up'). What does this
'lifted up' refer to? Is it to his death? To his resurrection? Possibly even his ascension? In my view, the correct answer to all of these questions is 'yes'. The lifting
up of Jesus on the cross, his lifting out of the tomb and
his lifting into heaven all combine together to achieve the
completion of the salvation that Jesus came to bring.

When in John's Gospel Jesus breathes his last, he says
'it is finished', indicating that the work that he has come
to do has now reached its completion. God's great love
spilled into the world in the person of Jesus and came to
its glorious and victorious fulfilment when Jesus stretched
out his arms in love on the cross. What in human sight
was ignominious defeat, was, in divine sight, glorious victory; what in human sight was an event of the utmost
despair, was, in divine sight, a moment of perfect joy;
what in human sight was the end, was, in divine sight, the
completion that brought forth a new beginning.

The story of Jesus' death and resurrection in Matthew,
Mark and Luke is told from human perspective, in all
its misery, despair and hopelessness. The story of Jesus'
death and resurrection in John's Gospel is told more from
divine perspective, a perspective that speaks of God's
aching love for the world that can only be satisfied by

offering the greatest gift of all – his son. John's Gospel teaches us the importance of retraining our sight to see the world not as it appears to us, but as it appears to God – a world that to us can seem cruel and hopeless, but to God is one that calls out for love and transformation.

ᴄᴛᴖᴄ

Then the disciples returned to their homes. But Mary stood weeping outside the tomb. . .. she turned around and saw Jesus standing there, but she did not know that it was Jesus. Jesus said to her, 'Woman, why are you weeping? Whom are you looking for?' Supposing him to be the gardener, she said to him, 'Sir, if you have carried him away, tell me where you have laid him, and I will take him away.' Jesus said to her, 'Mary!' She turned and said to him in Hebrew, 'Rabbouni!' (which means Teacher).

John 20.10–16

Our eyes, the sense that many of us rely on more than all the others, can be incredibly unreliable, or at least what our brain does with what we see can be unreliable. As a rule I have an excellent memory for faces but a terrible memory for names. I can see someone, especially if they are out of context, know that I know them but can spend the whole conversation with them trying to work out in my head why I know them and where I last met them. The signals my eyes send to my brain are good but partial.

In both Luke's and John's accounts of resurrection there are issues with sight. One of the intriguing questions is why the two on the road to Emmaus, and Mary in the garden did not recognize Jesus when they saw him.

One option is that Jesus' resurrection body looked so different from his pre-resurrection body that they could not recognize him. This raises questions of continuity and discontinuity. There is enough continuity between the pre-resurrection Jesus and the post resurrection Jesus for his body still to bear the scars of his death (the holes in his hands and feet) but enough discontinuity for his face to be different. Another option is that he looked no different but that because neither the two nor Mary expected to see him they simply didn't recognize him.

It is almost impossible to decide which one of these options is the more likely because the text tells us too little to help us decide. What is clear is that both the two on the road to Emmaus and Mary needed additional help to recognize Jesus. At Emmaus it was the act of hospitality that led to the point of recognition in the breaking of the bread; with Mary it was Jesus' voice that allowed her to see Jesus for who he was. All of this reminds us of how unreliable our eyes can be. Perhaps it is because it is too easy: we look and draw quick conclusions without allowing the rest of ourselves to catch up. Sometimes what we need to do is to see with inner sight, rather than just outer sight. Mary had to get to the stage where she perceived Jesus in a different way (in this case by hearing his voice) for her to comprehend who he was.

I suspect that Mary is not alone in this. Part of the Christian journey of faith is this re-training of our senses so that we can see truly and hear fully, not only God in our midst but also in the world around us. In Mark's Gospel when the disciples had misunderstood, yet one more time, what Jesus was saying he asked them, 'Do you have eyes, and fail to see? Do you have ears, and fail to hear? And do you not remember?' (Mark 8.18). The answer to this question is all too often yes – yes we have eyes and do not see, yes ears and do not hear and we do not remember. The question which resounds for me from this story is: If Jesus simply spoke my name, as he did Mary's, would I hear and recognize him or would it take much more than that?

෴

Then he said to Thomas, 'Put your finger here and see my hands. Reach out your hand and put it in my side. Do not doubt but believe.' Thomas answered him, 'My Lord and my God!' Jesus said to him, 'Have you believed because you have seen me? Blessed are those who have not seen and yet have come to believe.'

John 20.27–9

For further reading: John 20.21–31

There's nothing in life that people love more than a stereotype. If we can pigeonhole someone, then we know how to deal with them on all occasions and how to react to them. Even if they surprise us and react in a new way, then we can say that it was unusual, a person like that would never normally do that. Anyone who has been on the receiving end of such a stereotype will tell you how debilitating and draining of life it can be. It hems them in, chains them to a certain way of being which they find hard to throw off. Not only that, but it can also cause those who do it to read a person almost entirely wrongly.

If any biblical character suffers under a stereotype it is surely Thomas, or to give him his usual name 'doubting Thomas'. Before we even encounter, Thomas we know what to think of him, how to react to him and what he will be like. I have for a long time felt that this was unfair. Thomas is a fascinating mixture of doubt and fervent belief; to write him off as 'doubting' is to underestimate him. Thomas appears three times in John's Gospel. The first time we meet him, Jesus is on his way to raise Lazarus from the dead. The disciples are urging him not to go because the Jews have recently tried to stone him (John 11.8) and Thomas declares that they should go so that 'we may die with him' (John 11.16). The second time, Jesus is talking about his Father's house in which there are many mansions, that he is going there to prepare a place for them and that they know the way. At this point Thomas bursts out with 'Lord, we do not know where you are going. How can we know the way?' (John 14.5). And then finally, here, after the resurrection, Thomas refuses to believe until he has seen the risen Jesus with his own eyes.

If we remove the stereotype from Thomas and encounter him as he truly is, then we discover not someone who believes too little (as the epithet 'doubting Thomas' suggests) but someone who believes passionately, deeply and with the whole of their being. In chapter 11, Thomas is prepared to go with Jesus to his death, when the others are concerned about his returning to Judea. Later, in chapter 14, he is so concerned to be with Jesus that his question about knowing the way bursts from him with frustration when he doesn't comprehend where Jesus is going. After the resurrection, he wants to see Jesus for himself but when he does, is the first person in any of the Gospel accounts to work out what this means and to proclaim 'My Lord and my God'. Where the others are still working out that Jesus is risen, Thomas has recognized it, understood it and proclaimed its meaning. Thomas only appears doubting because it matters so much to him; once he has worked out what it means, he is the clearest, most fervent believer of all. It is high time for Thomas to be allowed to throw off his stereotype and become the 'passionate, believing Thomas' he really was.

Simon Peter said to them, 'I am going fishing.' They said to him, 'We will go with you.' They went out and got into the boat, but that night they caught nothing. Just after daybreak, Jesus stood on the beach; but the disciples did not know that it was Jesus. Jesus said to them, 'Children, you have no fish, have you?' They answered him, 'No.' He said to them, 'Cast the net to the right side of the boat, and you will find some.' So they cast it, and now they were not able to haul it in because there were so many fish. . . Jesus said to them, 'Come and have breakfast.' Now none of the disciples dared to ask him, 'Who are you?' because they knew it was the Lord. Jesus came and took the bread and gave it to them, and did the same with the fish.

John 21.3–6 and 12–13

For further reading: John 21.1–14

Why do you think Simon Peter decided to go fishing at this particular moment? One possibility is that its a sign that he has given up and gone back to his old job. The other is that he was ill at ease and, being a fisherman by trade, sought to calm himself by doing what he knew best – fishing – though how restful and calming it would have been to fish all night and catch nothing is another question entirely. Maybe he was even trying to reassure himself that he wasn't a failure at everything (although on this night he also fails at fishing!).

It is important not to confuse this story with Luke's similar story, which took place when Jesus first called Simon, James and John. In that story, Simon and the others had been fishing all night and caught nothing, a point that Simon drew Jesus' attention to before doing as he was asked. There the point of the story was that they had caught nothing and were frustrated, and Jesus provided for them. Here the lack of fish seems less important. What was more important was having something to eat for breakfast with Jesus.

Over the years commentators have been intrigued by the fact that 153 fish were caught and many have attempted to work out the significance of that precise number (so much so that there must be close to 153 explanations of the significance of the number 153). As so often, it is easy to miss the wood for the trees here. There may, of course, be a subtle and clever explanation for the number of fish being 153, but in looking for it we are in danger of missing the obvious. There were, we are told, seven disciples present (Simon Peter, Thomas, Nathanael, John, James and two unnamed disciples) plus Jesus. Even if they were all ravenously hungry after a night's fishing, the maximum that eight people could eat for breakfast would be what – 16, maybe even 24 fish? What this miracle is most reminiscent of is Jesus' very first miracle at the wedding in Cana (in John 2.1–11) where he made in the region of 120–180 gallons of wine towards the end of the wedding feast. Just as then Jesus provided ridiculous quantities of wine, so now he produces fantastic quantities of fish, far more than eight people could even hope to eat, even if they sat there all day.

The post-resurrection Jesus has not changed. His first miracle is just like his last and takes generosity to ridiculous lengths. I suspect that, when faced by this generosity, the disciples forgot their unease entirely and the reason they went fishing in the first place. Just as Jesus remained the same from the beginning to the ending of John's Gospel, so also he remains the same today, and loves nothing more than to distract us from our attempts to find calm with mind-boggling, unexpected demonstrations of generosity. We need to be careful not to spend so long trying to work out the significance of the precise form of generosity offered that we forget to enjoy what has been given.

ᴄ⳼ᴐ

When they had finished breakfast, Jesus said to Simon Peter, 'Simon son of John, do you love me more than these?' He said to him, 'Yes, Lord; you know that I love you.' Jesus said to him, 'Feed my lambs.' A second time he said to him, 'Simon son of John, do you love me?' He said to him, 'Yes, Lord; you know that I love you.' Jesus said to him, 'Tend my sheep.' He said to him the third time, 'Simon son of John, do you love me?' Peter felt hurt because he said to him the third time, 'Do you love me?' And he said to him, 'Lord, you know everything; you know that I love you.' Jesus said to him, 'Feed my sheep' . . . After this he said to him, 'Follow me.'

John 21.15–17 and 19

At what point does gentle reminding turn into nagging? If we were able to answer this question clearly and straightforwardly then many relationships would be saved from a huge amount of grief. Unfortunately, most of us only know the answer to this question after the event. That 2nd/10th/59th time (delete as appropriate) was the reminder too far. Part of the complexity is that it is not the same answer every time. Sometimes and for some people the 2nd reminder is too much while for others and at other times this only happens with the 59th reminder.

In many situations Jesus' repeated questions to Peter would veer dangerously close to nagging, or at least rubbing his nose in it. Nevertheless, in this context three times was the perfect, in fact, the only number of times that would suffice. Peter's assurances of love and commitment to do as Jesus asked, needed to match exactly the number of times that he had denied Jesus. In exactly the measure that he had denied, Peter is invited to state his commitment, belief and loyalty. This is no nagging, this is love revealed in its most understanding form.

What is interesting is Jesus' response to Peter's declaration of love. We might expect any one of a number of commands: 'Do you love me? Believe in me' or 'Do you love me? Stand by me in times of trial' or again 'Do you love me? Show your loyalty.' Instead, the command turns Peter outwards. His expression of love is not to show piety or worship to Jesus but to care for Jesus' flock. In our modern world, the word love has become almost entirely associated with emotion. 'Do you love me?' is a question that asks for a response based on feeling. In the ancient world, emotion was important, but not as important as action. Many times in the Bible the command to love involves doing something. So, for example, in Romans 12.10 the command to love ('love one another with mutual affection' is joined with a command to action ('outdo one another in showing honour'). The same is true here: Peter is to show his love not by emotion alone but by caring for Jesus' lambs, he is to love Jesus by feeding and nurturing like a shepherd.

Jesus' final command to Peter ('follow me' 21.19) may seem odd at this point in Jesus' ministry but reminds us of the Good Shepherd in John 10.27, where Jesus, as Good

Shepherd, states, 'I know them and they follow me'. Peter's third and final response to Jesus' questioning is 'you know everything, you know that I love you' (21.17), his best response then is to follow. Even more importantly for Peter, Jesus is implicitly affirming that he knows of Peter's love: 'I know them and they follow me', that is, 'I know you and your love, now follow me.' Jesus tells Peter that he does know everything about him both good and bad, both his love and his denial, but he is still to follow and that following finds its expression not just in trailing after the Shepherd but in caring for the Shepherd's flock.

Concluding reflections

If Mark's Gospel is in danger of covering too little of the resurrection, John's is in danger of covering it too much. Whereas in Mark Jesus never appears to the disciples; in John he appears over and over again: to individuals and to groups, as proof of his resurrection and to commission. These appearances call forth recognition and response (Mary cries 'Teacher' and Thomas 'My Lord and my God') but also a sending outwards in proclamation and loving care for the world. The point of recognizing Jesus is not, like that of recognizing a celebrity (so that we can feel personally pleased to have met them), but so that the light might shine further allowing more and more people to see and comprehend God's love for the world. After his denial, Peter is drawn back into relationship with Jesus not so that he could feel better, or even bask in his love of Jesus, but so that he can go on to show that love by taking tender care of the other members of the flock. Unlike

Mark, John leaves us in no doubt of what will happen next, as we, like Peter, follow the Shepherd who knows us through and through and care for his flock.

5

RAISED FROM THE
DEAD

The Resurrection and the Epistles

Introduction

I approach this section of the book with a certain level of
trepidation. People who read the New Testament are gen-
erally split into two camps: those who love the writings of
Paul and those who cannot stand them. Those who love
the writings of Paul may well have a personal list of texts
that they would like me to look at (which I don't); those
who do not might prefer me to skip straight over to the
ascension. Nevertheless, for me it is vitally important in
a book that is exploring the resurrection to look at what
Paul has to say. Paul was the first – and probably greatest
– writer of the earliest Christian period who attempted
not just to describe *what* happened but what it meant
(and in fact continues to mean). It is Paul's writings on
resurrection that begin to give us a sense of why the resurrection is so very important in Christian theology. The
choices of passage that I have made reflect what I think
are his important discussions of resurrection focusing on
Jesus' resurrection, our own resurrection, God's action in
raising Jesus from the dead and how this all transforms
our lives as Christians.

This section contains 12 reflections, ten based on the Pauline writings, one based on Hebrews and one on 1 Peter. I wanted to make this chapter genuinely drawn from all the Epistles – not just from Paul – but there are few references to the resurrection outside the Pauline epistles and so I decided to use just two. Somewhat inevitably this chapter is more ideas based (since Paul and the other authors of the Epistles didn't really tell stories) and more disparate (because ideas on the resurrection are spread throughout the Epistles and not themed according to narrative). I have arranged them according to the order they appear in the New Testament.

Paul, probably more than any other writer, assumes that our fate after death will be resurrection. If you have not read the introduction, you might like now to read just the section called 'Resurrection and life after death' to help you understand what Paul means by this and how we can understand it today.

Therefore his faith 'was reckoned to him as righteousness.' Now the words, 'it was reckoned to him,' were written not for his sake alone, but for ours also. It will be reckoned to us who believe in him who raised Jesus our Lord from the dead, who was handed over to death for our trespasses and was raised for our justification.

Romans 4.22–5

For further reading: Romans 4.22—5.9

A while ago I had a conversation with someone who was a new Christian and was trying to make sense of what she had heard in church. She asked me what the resurrection was for. She had been coming to church for a while and she understood nearly all of the Christian festivals (including Good Friday) but she simply couldn't understand why we needed Easter. 'Is it' she asked me, 'simply so that we can be cheerful after a long Lent and depressing Good Friday? Didn't Jesus do everything he needed to do on the cross to save us? Did he really need to rise from the dead?' Such questions are dangerous ones to address to me and she went away a long time later, weighed down with much theology – though not necessarily much wiser!

I was intrigued, however, that she should have picked this up so soon because on one level she was right. One could be excused for thinking that the death and resurrection of Jesus were unconnected in terms of theology (the cross being about salvation, and resurrection about life now and in the world to come) and that the cross was, in fact, more important than the resurrection. I suspect that this was partially what lay behind the woman's questions – she was flummoxed by being told that Easter was the most important day in the Christian year but feeling that somehow Good Friday was more significant.

Throughout Christian history great – and appropriate – emphasis has been placed on Jesus' death on the cross as the means by which we enter into a new relationship with God, based not on law but on faith. Sometimes, however, one could be forgiven for wondering whether Jesus needed to rise from the dead at all, if everything has already been achieved in its entirety by his dying. Would it have made any significant difference to salvation if Jesus died for our sins and remained dead? For me the answer is yes, it would make an enormous difference.

Scholars counsel against making too much of Paul's distinction in Romans 4.25 between the effect of Jesus' death (for our trespasses) and the effect of his resurrection (for our justification). Paul does not often make this distinction in his writings and we should not over-emphasize it here. Nevertheless, his phrase in verse 25 reminds us that the death and resurrection of Jesus are intimately linked. If any distinction can be made between the two, then roughly speaking Jesus' death frees us 'from' and his resurrection frees us 'for': from our sins, for a life in Christ; from our old way of being, for new creation and so on. By and large, however, the death and resurrection of Jesus should be seen as a seamless whole working together for our salvation. We need both Good Friday and Easter Day, death and resurrection. One without the other would be very much impoverished.

Do you not know that all of us who have been baptized into Christ Jesus were baptized into his death? Therefore we have been buried with him by baptism into death, so that, just as Christ was raised from the dead by the glory of the Father, so we too might walk in newness of life. For if we have been united with him in a death like his, we will certainly be united with him in a resurrection like his.

Romans 6.3–5

For further reading: Romans 6.1–11

Trying to explain baptism to a child is something of a challenge. I once overheard a conversation between a mother and her son at a baptism service which rather summed up the problem. It went a little like this: 'Mum, why is that man putting water on the baby?' 'He's baptizing her?' 'Oh, what is that?' 'He is welcoming her into God's family?' 'With water?' 'Yes.' 'If I have a bath does that make me a part of our family?' 'No you are a part of our family already.' 'So he's washing her?' 'Yes.' 'Why was she dirty?' At this point the mother gave up, and with clever sleight of hand distracted the child onto something else, but the question remains. What does baptism do?

In Romans 6 Paul gives one of the best explanations of the nature of baptism that we can hope to find. In this passage Paul sees baptism as a way of mimicking the death and resurrection of Christ. In Paul's image the water is to be seen as symbolizing death and burial. As we go down into the water we die and are buried with Christ; as we come out of the water we rise with him into newness of life. In baptism, therefore, we come to share in the life of Christ, dying and rising with him so that we might now live a new Christ-like life.

Paul's theology of baptism makes it clear that Jesus' resurrection is no longer just *his* resurrection, it is now the resurrection of us all. When Jesus rose from the dead he opened up a new way of being in which the characteristics of our own future resurrection life (which will happen at the end of the world) are now available – in part – to those who are in Christ. When we are baptized we follow in the footsteps of Christ and enter that new creation. This is where we begin to see that, rather than being an interesting historical event, Jesus' resurrection is something that affects everything that we do. 'This risen existence', as R. S. Thomas so evocatively calls it, is not just Jesus' own risen existence but yours and mine too. We live resurrection lives – lives transformed by a new creation.

Before we leave this passage we need to pause for a moment over the question of the practicalities of baptism. For many people the issue of full immersion versus pouring water over the head or infant versus adult baptism are faith-defining questions. We need to acknowledge, however, that Paul gives us no easy answers to these questions, either here or elsewhere. Any answers we arrive at will be derivative, that is, we will have to work them out from the incomplete, insubstantial and partial references that exist within the Bible and, as often happens in these cases, widely different conclusions will be drawn using the same evidence. People who pour water on babies' heads in baptism can justify this approach from the Bible just as those who immerse adults can. The problem is that the practice of baptism is one of those thorny subjects that can easily occupy us for hours on end and so distract us from the substance of what Paul is talking about here. What is most important is not *how* we baptize but *that* by doing so we we join in with Christ's dying and rising. It is this that is transformative and that forms the bedrock for much of Paul's theology.

Now if Christ is proclaimed as raised from the dead, how can some of you say there is no resurrection of the dead? If there is no resurrection of the dead, then Christ has not been raised; and if Christ has not been raised, then our proclamation has been in vain and your faith has been in vain. We are even found to be misrepresenting God, because we testified of God that he raised Christ – whom he did not raise if it is true that the dead are not raised. For if the dead are not raised, then Christ has not been raised. If Christ has not been raised, your faith is futile and you are still in your sins.

1 Corinthians 15.12–17

For further reading: 1 Corinthians 15.1–19

This passage is a favourite sermon passage. Over the years I have heard this passage preached on many, many times and on the vast majority of those occasions it was used to prove the truth of Jesus' resurrection. By and large, the sermons I have heard focus on the iconic phrase 'If Christ has not been raised, your faith is futile and you are still in your sins' (1 Corinthians 15.17). Central as this phrase is to Paul's argument here, it is not included in order to persuade the Corinthians of Jesus' resurrection. There seems to be no hint in Paul's argument that they had any doubts on this front. Their question seems to have been about what would happen to them after they died. In the first century there was a wide variety of views about what happened after you died ranging from belief in nothing at all to the idea of the transmigration of the soul (that is, the body died but the soul lived on and, after spending time in Hades, entered another human body). Resurrection – the idea that at some point in the future your body would be raised to life and transformed so that you would live for ever – was a peculiarly Jewish idea and would have been alien to anyone of Graeco-Roman heritage. Given the other disputes that were going on in the Corinthian Christian community, the most likely scenario here is that the Corinthians accepted Jesus' death and resurrection but held to their own previous, Graeco-Roman-inspired beliefs about what would happen to them after death.

Paul explains to them that this is not an option. He reminds them that Jesus has been raised and gives them proof of this (15.1–11) and then points out that it is therefore illogical to say that resurrection does not happen: to do that would be to chop off the theological branch upon which the whole of their faith rested. If you want to believe that Jesus has been raised from the dead, then you must also believe that others will be raised as well; if you say there is no resurrection, you are also saying that Jesus did not rise.

Contemporary Christians have different – and even more acute – problems. Today, numerous people believe neither in Jesus' resurrection nor their own. For them to be told that not believing in the general resurrection of the dead undermines their belief in Jesus' resurrection, would be no problem at all. Nevertheless, Paul's point remains. Without resurrection of any kind, our faith changes: resurrection affects the doctrine of hope, of Christian identity, of baptism, of life after death, and also of God. Resurrection is the thread that is woven right through the centre of many of our Christian beliefs. Those who wish to pull out that thread need to recognize how much of the pattern of Christian faith also comes away. They may still want to do it but then are faced with a huge challenge of re-envisioning Christianity. Taking out the resurrection is not like taking off a small block of stone from the top of a wall; it is more like taking out a large, load-bearing stone from the bottom. It can be done, but you will need to do a lot of shoring up of other things if you do.

⁕

There are both heavenly bodies and earthly bodies, but the glory of the heavenly is one thing, and that of the earthly is another. There is one glory of the sun, and another glory of the moon, and another glory of the stars; indeed, star differs from star in glory. So it is with the resurrection of the dead. What is sown is perishable, what is raised is imperishable. It is sown in dishonor, it is raised in glory. It is sown in weakness, it is raised in power. It is sown a physical body, it is raised a spiritual body. If there is a physical body, there is also a spiritual body.

1 Corinthians 15.40–4

For further reading: 1 Corinthians 15.20–58

Sometime ago someone asked me whether I liked my body and the question stumped me entirely. I had no idea. I don't dislike it. Is that the same as liking it? The question and my reaction to it has stayed with me ever since. My own reaction intrigued me as much as the question. I felt pleased with myself that I could say that I didn't dislike my body. On reflection, however, it is somewhat shocking that I could think that not disliking my body was in anyway a positive statement. Imagine if someone had asked me whether I liked my friends – if I said I didn't dislike them, I could be pretty sure to become friendless rather quickly.

Christian tradition has been, for a long time, at best, ambivalent about bodies and, at worst, antagonistic towards them and everything that they represent. This ambivalence/antagonism can also be found more widely in society. So often the media present the body-perfect with the implication that anything less than perfection is to be despised. Anorexia, obesity and dieting abound as people feel increasingly bad about the bodies they have. Whether this attitude towards bodies finds its roots in the Christian tradition or in consumer culture, or both, there is an urgent need for us to rethink bodies and our attitudes towards them.

The person often blamed for this negativity towards bodies is Paul, who so often seems to contrast the things of the flesh with the things of the spirit. The natural assumption is that bodies are bad and the spirit is good. This particular part of 1 Corinthians challenges us to lay down all our presuppositions about bodies, flesh, spirit, soul and what Paul thought about them, and pick them up again in a different order. We can only really understand Paul's attitude to the body if we comprehend that he believed in bodily resurrection. It is not bodies, per se, that Paul has a problem with but the current age and everything shaped by it. For Paul, the problem is not with bodies but bodies of the present time. Resurrection bodies are different altogether.

Thus, in this passage he contrasts the bodies we have now with the bodies we will have when we are raised. Paul offers four contrasts between our bodies. Our current bodies are decaying, humiliated, weak and confined to this realm; our risen bodies will be vigorous, splendid, powerful and fit for the realm of the spirit** (15.42–3) *but* they will still be bodies. Paul does not say that our current bodies are evil, as some might expect him to, simply that they are to our resurrection bodies what the moon is to the sun. They are not to be despised but are to be replaced by something far, far more glorious than before. Jesus' resurrection brings us into a new relationship with many things, including our bodies. Our current bodies may be sagging, creaking and wrinkling before our eyes but they are not to be hated. This risen existence requires us to learn to live well in our bodies now because, once raised from the dead, we will have a body – albeit a different glorious one – for eternity.

❧

* The NRSV translation is not hugely helpful here as it implies a contrast between physical and spiritual bodies (that is, that our risen bodies will not be physical). The real contrast is between physical bodies bound by material things and those enlivened by spiritual things.

For while we live, we are always being given up to death for Jesus' sake, so that the life of Jesus may be made visible in our mortal flesh. So death is at work in us, but life in you. But just as we have the same spirit of faith that is in accordance with scripture – 'I believed, and so I spoke' – we also believe, and so we speak, because we know that the one who raised the Lord Jesus will raise us also with Jesus, and will bring us with you into his presence.

2 Corinthians 4.11–14

For further reading: 2 Corinthians 4.7–18

My husband's uncle, who was ordained, used to describe visits to some people as the 'organ recital', and it is easy to see what he meant. The simple question 'How are you?' can, in some cases, lead to a long recitation of what is wrong with someone's organs (liver, kidneys, stomach, heart and so on). There are people that I do my best to avoid asking how they are lest I be pinned to the spot for the next hour or so while they tell me in minute detail *precisely* how they are.

It can feel sometimes as though Paul is a little like this. Particularly in 2 Corinthians, he seems to go to town when talking about suffering, weakness and mishaps (if shipwrecks can be called mishaps!). Nevertheless, there is a difference, which this passage makes clear. Those who love to tell you of their illnesses want you to focus on them and them alone; Paul wants us to focus on Christ. For Paul, the recounting of his various disasters is deliberate in order to turn the Corinthians' attention from him to Christ. Over and over again in 2 Corinthians Paul returns to this theme that what the Corinthians see as despicable weakness is the way in which they – and the world as a

{75}

whole – may encounter more fully the glory of Christ.

In this passage Paul talks about the difference that the resurrection makes to him. The straightforward difference is one that we encountered in 1 Corinthians 15. Paul has the confidence to speak of what he believes (4.13) because he knows that the God who raised Jesus from the dead will also raise both Paul and the Corinthians. Quite simply, for Paul Jesus' resurrection is the proof of his own: if God can do it for Jesus, he is confident God can do it for him – Paul – as well.

In a more complex train of thought, Paul sees his own sufferings as the way in which Christ's resurrection life can shine forth. One of the basic characteristics of human nature is the drive to survive at all costs. Jesus laid down that 'right' to fight for his own survival in order to ensure survival for us. What Paul is saying here is that he too is prepared to lay down his fight for survival and by doing so allows the vigorous, splendid, powerful resurrected life of Christ to shine through his decaying, humiliated, weak, mortal body. He will, at some point, receive his own glorious resurrected body, but for now he is content for Christ's resurrected life to shine from him. Thus, paradoxically, in being given up to death he can bring life to the Corinthians. Jesus put this in different terms but with the same meaning: 'those who want to save their life will lose it, and those who lose their life for my sake, and for the sake of the gospel, will save it' (Mark 8.35).

This fundamental Christian message is one that we still struggle with. It goes against every human instinct to embrace weakness rather than strength and failure rather than success but this apparent contradiction lies at the heart of the Christian gospel. To use an earlier image from 2 Corinthians 4.7, Christ's light can only really shine properly through cracked, crumbling clay jars; nicely finished, properly glazed jars would keep the light in and simply allow people to say what nice jars they are. The jars need to be cracked for Christ's light to be able shine through. One of the hardest challenges we face as Christians is to let this lesson sink from our heads into our emotions and onwards into our Christian practice. Everything in us shies away from weakness and failure. Learning to live a true risen existence involves also learning to live fully and joyfully as cracked and crumbling clay jars.

❧

So if anyone is in Christ, there is a new creation: everything old has passed away; see, everything has become new! All this is from God, who reconciled us to himself through Christ, and has given us the ministry of reconciliation; that is, in Christ God was reconciling the world to himself, not counting their trespasses against them, and entrusting the message of reconciliation to us.

2 Corinthians 5.17–19

For further reading: 2 Corinthians 5.11–21

It is hard these days not to feel a little cynical about the 'new'. We are bombarded with enticements to get new things with the underlying message that the new thing we have got will be so much better than the old that our lives will be transformed as a result. My family recently got the game 'Connect 4', which had emblazoned on the front 'new Connect 4'. As far as I could see it was almost exactly the same as old Connect 4 but made with cheaper plastic.

What then do we make of Paul's talk of 'new creation'? Does this fall into the category of 'new stuff' that replaces the old whether it was broken or not and promises much that it cannot deliver? Hardly surprisingly, I would say no. New creation is an entirely different kind of 'newness', genuinely new and greatly needed. For me, this is one of those essential Pauline passages that encapsulates a lot of what we need to know. What Paul is doing here is talking about how the world is different now that Christ has risen from the dead. For Paul, Christ's death and resurrection didn't only change Christ but changes us as well. When Christ rose from the dead, a new way of being was opened up, which was not governed by the material things of this age but by the things of God. For the first time, then, it became possible for human beings to throw off the old life and all that governed it and enter a new life, governed by the Spirit. The phrase Paul uses to express this is being 'in Christ'. If we are 'in Christ' we now have a new identity shaped no longer by the human impulses that we cannot control but by Christ and all he was and did.

Being in Christ is truly to be a 'new creation', with a newness that it both genuinely new and genuinely needed. This hugely important verse in 2 Corinthians 5.17 is, however, somewhat difficult to translate. The Greek simply says: 'if anyone in Christ, new creation'. Our English translations struggle to put it into good English: some have 'if anyone is in Christ, he is a new creation', others have 'if anyone is in Christ, there is a new creation'. The two are crucially different and I suspect are both correct. Anyone who is in Christ is newly created with a new Christ-like identity that transforms everything that they do. At the same time, if anyone is in Christ, new creation now exists. In other words, the new heaven and new earth that the book of Revelation speaks of as coming at the end of time, have already come into being. It is not only we who are transformed, but the world as well.

As Paul says in 5.19, in Christ God was reconciling the world to himself. This is no simple personal reconciliation but a glorious cosmic one. It is now possible to be fully and deeply at one with God, with one another and with the created order. This is one of the reasons that Paul feels so deeply grieved at the conflict that exists in Christian communities. The marker of the new creation that exists in Christ is not conflict but reconciliation, a reconciliation that spreads outwards from those in Christ to the world around. This is a message that is as vital today as it has ever been, if only we can hear it.

Paul an apostle – sent neither by human commission nor from human authorities, but through Jesus Christ and God the Father, who raised him from the dead –

Galatians 1.1

When I was a child we used to go on holiday every year to a small village right in the middle of Wales where there were so many people with the surname Jones that people had to describe them further. So the farm on which we stayed was owned by Jones the farm, the postman was Jones the post, the shopkeeper, Jones the shop and so on. It was an immensely efficient way of identifying people, not least because you discovered both their name and what they did straight away. Adding an epithet to their name not only helped to identity them but also told you a little about them.

In Paul's writings, one of the more common epithets given to God is the 'God who raised Jesus from the dead', which we find in various different forms one of which is here in Galatians 1.1. This epithet is important for a number of reasons. It clearly establishes the uniqueness of God in Paul's context, where there were a number of gods known by various characteristics, such as Aphrodite, goddess of love, Artemis the goddess of fertility and so on. The characteristic of raising Jesus from the dead gives God a unique identification not known among any of the other gods of Paul's day.

It is also important for another reason. For Paul, Jesus' resurrection was an event – an event that transforms our lives – but it also became a divine characteristic, something that tells us about God's nature. First, it tells us something about God's capacity to act in the world. This is not a God who sets the world in motion and steps back, but a God who not only can but did intervene to the extent that he performed the impossible. Not only did he bring the dead to life but he collapsed the boundaries of time, so that an event that should only have happened at the end of time occurred right in the middle of it.

The other thing that resurrection tells us about the nature of God is that nothing, absolutely nothing is beyond the life-giving creative love of God. We might think that the murder of an innocent man, in the most gruesome way possible, was beyond even God's redemptive love, but it was not. This God is the kind of God who can take even that horrific event and from it bring new life and new hope. It is this characteristic that we can cling to in the storms that afflict our own lives. As Christians, however hard things are and however bad we feel, there is always hope built firmly on the foundations of the God who raised Jesus from the dead.

The challenge for us is, if God is this kind of God, what kind of Christians are we? In prayer and worship the deep essence of God speaks to our inner beings, transforming us and making us more like him. If God is the kind of God who breathes new life and new hope into a dying and hopeless world, then we who worship him must be the same. Christians ought to be the kind of people to whom others look for creativity, new life, hope and a better future. This was partially why Paul became so exasperated with Christians in Galatia, Corinth and elsewhere when they became self-centred and inward-looking. So often, even from the start, the Christian community has hidden rather than revealed the God who raised Jesus from the dead. Being Easter people, children of the resurrection, requires us to be people whose own characteristics match those of the God who brings new life where there is only death, and hope where there is only despair.

... with the eyes of your heart enlightened, you may know what is the hope to which he has called you, what are the riches of his glorious inheritance among the saints, and what is the immeasurable greatness of his power for us who believe, according to the working of his great power. God put this power to work in Christ when he raised him from the dead and seated him at his right hand in the heavenly places ... And he has put all things under his feet and has made him the head over all things for the church, which is his body, the fullness of him who fills all in all.

Ephesians 1.17–20 and 22–3

For further reading: Ephesians 1.17–23

One of the things that human beings are bad at is recognizing how very fortunate we are. I recently read a book with a highly entertaining premise. It was called *The Year of Living Biblically* by A. J. Jacobs, a non-practising Jew who, as the title suggests, spent a year trying to obey every single command in the Hebrew scriptures. It is quite tongue in cheek and I particularly enjoyed his ruminations on whether dropping a pebble onto the shoe of an adulterer technically counted as stoning them or not. It raises all sorts of questions about how we engage with laws and what keeping laws really means, but for me the most moving thing about the book is that the author learnt how to be thankful. One of the major features of keeping the law is giving thanks and Jacobs discovered that the discipline of giving thanks made him see the world in an entirely new light.

The last thing that Paul would ever suggest would be that we, Gentiles, all rush off to keep the law as a way of becoming thankful, but underneath this passage lies a similar kind of theme. Paul wishes that the eyes of the Ephesians' hearts might be enlightened so that they can know the hope of God's calling, the riches of his inheritance of glory and the greatness of his power, which is beyond comprehension (which is another way of translating 'the immeasurable greatness of his power'), a power that was revealed in Jesus' resurrection and ascension. This power is not hidden from them nor newly available in the present time, but is what is on offer permanently to the Ephesians – and also to us. In fact, their very existence as a Christian community is thanks to this resurrected and ascended Jesus who is now head of the Church. The implications of what Paul says is that it belongs to them – and has done since they became a church – but they simply don't recognize it. They, like us, fail to see the immeasurable wealth of what God has to give.

There is a passage in C. S. Lewis's book, *The Last Battle,* when most people have passed through the door of the stable into 'new Narnia', that is, the world to come. Alongside many other people who have gone through the door are some dwarves who sit on the luscious green grass of the newly created world and complain about their poor lot. They are in the new world but all they can see is a dirty old stable with rubbish on the floor. So often, we have a tendency to be like the dwarves. We are inheritors of the most incredible gifts from God and yet all we can see is problems. Part of the resurrection life involves recognizing the astounding gifts that God has given us and learning to give thanks. Living thankful lives takes practice. Too often we learn the skills of cynicism and pessimism, which squeeze out the apparently less sophisticated skill of thankfulness. Living the resurrection life in all its fullness requires us to engage in the discipline of thankfulness that begins deep down in our hearts and bubbles outwards to everything that we do.

But God, who is rich in mercy, out of the great love with which he loved us even when we were dead through our trespasses, made us alive together with Christ – by grace you have been saved – and raised us up with him and seated us with him in the heavenly places in Christ Jesus, so that in the ages to come he might show the immeasurable riches of his grace in kindness toward us in Christ Jesus ... For we are what he has made us, created in Christ Jesus for good works, which God prepared beforehand to be our way of life.

Ephesians 2.4–7 and 10

For further reading: Ephesians 2.1–10

Do mixed metaphors entertain or irritate you? I am obliged to be entertained by them, since I am probably one of the worst culprits when it comes to mixing metaphors. It makes me feel better to discover that I'm not alone. There are various lists of them to be found and my favourites include: 'We could stand here talking until the cows turn blue'; 'I wouldn't eat that with a ten-foot pole' and 'it's as easy as falling off a piece of cake'. Even the great orator Barack Obama is attributed with saying, 'As we consider the road that unfolds before us . . .' Mixed metaphors are always a risk for anyone who attempts to use images to bring what they are saying to life.

Paul is no different. We could be forgiven here for feeling a little confused. Didn't Paul say in Romans 6.3–5 that in our baptism we die and rise with Christ? How then can he say here that we were already dead in our sins? If, in our baptism we die with Christ, surely we cannot already have been dead? The answer, of course, as with all passages in Paul, is that Paul was using various images to explain his profound – and frankly complicated – message. Surely we can forgive him a few over-intricate images?

In Romans 6.3–5 he is talking about the process of how we die with Christ and rise again; whereas here he is contrasting the pre-'in Christ' state with the post-'in Christ' state. Before we were in Christ we were effectively 'dead in our sins'. The only 'cure' for death is resurrection. If we were previously dead in our sins, then the image that works best to explain that we are now alive is resurrection. Paul is not so much guilty of mixed metaphors as of using the same metaphor to describe two different things.

This is one of those passages where Paul begins to unpack what impact the resurrection has on our day-to-day lives. If we have been made alive with Christ, then our identity is bound up with him and with his risen existence. We have been remade by God, recreated in Christ. As a result, we are no longer the people we were before but are reshaped and remade as Christ-like beings, recreated for 'good works'. Acting well is now a part of who we are. It is not something we can choose to do or not to do depending on how we feel. It is a part of our nature as newly created beings. Not doing good works would be like being created to walk on two legs and opting instead to go on all fours.

Our new identity in Christ involves an odd mixture of nature and nurture. Our identity changes but this also requires an act of will on our part. God has now created us differently and we can choose to embrace this new identity or to ignore it. The choice is ours but we should be clear that ignoring it also involves rejecting Jesus' resurrection, God's action in raising of Jesus from the dead and our own future resurrection. The resurrection is not an interesting fact but something that demands in us a complete change of outlook. It is the ultimate Monday morning theology: true, it is theology, but unless it transforms what we do and how we think on Monday mornings (as well as every other day of the week) it is of no value whatsoever.

❧

So if you have been raised with Christ, seek the things that are above, where Christ is, seated at the right hand of God. Set your minds on things that are above, not on things that are on earth, for you have died, and your life is hidden with Christ in God. When Christ who is your life is revealed, then you also will be revealed with him in glory. Put to death, therefore, whatever in you is earthly: fornication, impurity, passion, evil desire, and greed (which is idolatry).

Colossians 3.1–5

For further reading: Colossians 3.1–15

The only place to end our exploration of Pauline reflections about resurrection is Colossians where Paul states explicitly what we have gleaned elsewhere. If we have been raised with Christ then we have a new identity, rooted and built up in him (as Paul says in Colossians 2.7). We are newly created, different human beings. As we saw in the previous passage from Ephesians, we have now been created for good works and must therefore live our lives with that in mind. As we saw in the passage above, our change of identity does not, unfortunately, come with an automatic change of behaviour. How nice it would be if one day we were consumed by greediness, selfishness and thoughtlessness, and on the next we skipped around with our minds centred solely on God and his mission for the world. You don't need me to tell you that this is not the way things are.

Rather, as Paul makes clear in this passage, living a new life in Christ involves resolve, setting our minds to it and working at it day by day. Being a Christian is not a cast-iron guarantee that we will be freed from all temptations and failures. Becoming Christ-like involves hard graft. It is a lifetime's activity that will still require further work even as we breathe our last. Paul tells us to seek the things above and to set our minds on them (Colossians 3.1–2). This is not like doing a U-turn in the car, where one moment we face in one direction and the next we face in the opposite direction, before driving off into the sunset. It is more like moving your socks from one drawer to another (multiplied by at least one hundred). When

you first move your socks, you go to the old drawer every
time to look for your socks. After a while, some of the
time you remember and go to the new drawer, and for the
rest of the time you forget. Then slowly more and more
often you remember until you only rarely return to the
old draw in search of socks.

The Christian existence is a little like this, with time
it is possible to retrain our minds to the things above, at
least some of the time. What is frustrating, however, is
that we learn one lesson – at least partially – and then a
new one arises and we have to begin again. To return to
the sock draw analogy, you just about remember where
your socks are and someone moves your T-shirts and you
have to begin the whole process from scratch. Learning to
fix your mind on the things above takes time, dedication
and vision. Here Paul reminds us why we battle on and
don't give up: because our lives our hidden with Christ in
God. We are not just 'in Christ', our lives are now where
Christ is – hidden in the God who raised us with Christ
in the first place and whose being is solely and completely
holy. If that is not motivation enough to keep us going, it
is hard to imagine what might be.

❧

*Now may the God of peace, who brought back from
the dead our Lord Jesus, the great shepherd of the
sheep, by the blood of the eternal covenant, make you
complete in everything good so that you may do his
will, working among us that which is pleasing in his
sight, through Jesus Christ, to whom be the glory forever and ever. Amen.*

Hebrews 13.20–1

For further reading: Hebrews 13.18–25 (and if you like as well Isaiah 63.7–19)

The book of Hebrews only mentions resurrection explicitly once. It bubbles away beneath the surface implicitly throughout the whole book but is only once referred to directly – here in Hebrews 13.20. This book is a fascinating book for a number of reasons. It is rooted more firmly in its Jewish heritage than, perhaps, any other book of the New Testament and is also much more like a sermon than it is a letter. This is reinforced by the fact that it ends with a prayer (13.20–1) and only a few exhortations and greetings (13.22–5). As with many sermons the prayer at the end draws together a good number of the strands that run throughout the book in something that is close to, but not quite, a summary.

One of the most striking features of Hebrews is that it is steeped in the Old Testament. It was clearly written by someone who had the Old Testament running through their veins. This is one of the reasons why many Christians today struggle to understand it. We do not have the Old Testament in us, in the way that the author of Hebrews does. As a result, we miss some of the resonances that make the book so profound. In this particular passage it seems likely that Isaiah 63.11 lies behind the language that is used: 'Then they remembered the days of old, of Moses his servant. Where is the one who brought them up out of the sea with the shepherds of his flock?' There are two reasons for this. The first is that, rather than using the language of raising Jesus from the dead, language which after exploring ten Pauline passages on resurrection we would now be familiar with, the author of Hebrews uses different language of bringing or leading Jesus up from the dead. If we compare this with Isaiah 63.11 you will notice that there the same language is used for bringing the people of God up out of the sea. Add to this the reference in both Hebrews and Isaiah to shepherds of the sheep and it seems that the author has this passage in mind.

One of the things that is interesting about this – in comparison with Paul's writings – is that although Paul loved images and metaphors, he never attached any to the resurrection of Jesus (only to our own relationship with the resurrection). For Paul the resurrection was sufficiently self-explanatory not to need images to help explain it. The author of Hebrews, however, does attach an image to the resurrection – that of the Exodus. For him Jesus' resurrection is a new Exodus. Jesus has been brought up out of the dead just like the people of God were brought out from the Red Sea. They were brought out with their leaders, the shepherds of the sheep, but Jesus was brought out alone, the Great Shepherd, the leader above all leaders. For the author of Hebrews, then, the resurrection is the ultimate Exodus. When Jesus rose from the dead we became truly free as never before.

It is the God who brings people into freedom that the author addresses in this prayer, praying that he will complete us (the Greek word has resonances of 'repair' in it) so that we may do his will. True freedom, glorious resurrected Exodus freedom, is not about pleasing ourselves (which can be an imprisonment in itself) but about doing God's will, for in him there is perfect freedom.

❦

Blessed be the God and Father of our Lord Jesus Christ! By his great mercy he has given us a new birth into a living hope through the resurrection of Jesus Christ from the dead, and into an inheritance that is imperish-

able, undefiled, and unfading, kept in heaven for you,
who are being protected by the power of God through
faith for a salvation ready to be revealed in the last
time.

1 Peter 1.3–5

For further reading: 1 Peter 1.3–12

I have the gift of the gab. I am all too aware that I can talk
and talk and talk without pausing for significant breaths
in between sentences. It is a gift I seem to have passed on
to my children and I am now suffering the consequences
of them talking at me non-stop from morning until night;
it seems only right, in a way, that I should also experience
the effects of something that I inflict on others. However,
my abilities to speak non-stop, pale into insignificance
compared with Peter. 1 Peter 1.3–12 is a single sentence,
finely crafted to hang together, but even I can't read it
out in one go without taking a breath somewhere in the
middle. This whole passage is one of the most profound
summaries of the nature of God, of Jesus and our relationship with them to be found in the whole of the New
Testament. It hasn't got every piece of theology in it that
we might need but it does have a lot of them. It is a bit
like a banquet of many courses, served up on a single
plate.

In a very similar way to the writings of Paul, 1 Peter
establishes his theological premise, which includes the
resurrection, and then goes on to talk about the difference it makes – or should make – to the way in which we
live our lives. This single sentence (1.3–12) is where Peter
puts down the theological foundations that underpin everything that he goes on to say about who we are and how
we live our lives now. These opening few verses tell us

something very important indeed about Peter's theology: very like Paul, he sees the whole of the Christian existence in the light of Jesus' resurrection.

In some of the previous passages we have been paying attention to the images used to explain the ideas and it is worth exploring the image Peter uses here. Paul describes our current existence using the image of dying and rising, drawn directly from the resurrection; Peter has a similar idea but brings in a different image – that of giving birth. One of the striking features of this passage is the verb that Peter uses to describe how it is that we have a new and living hope: he says that God has given birth to us again. On one level this is very familiar and is like the image of being born again that we find in chapter 3 of John's Gospel. What is unusual here is that the verb is active not passive, focused more on God than on us. The passage could have said that 'we have been born again by God' or 'brought to new life by God', but it does not. Instead it says that God gave birth to us again or regenerated us. God is not a distant contributor to new life but an active labourer as he brings us into the new realm of life in Christ.

Peter has made the link here between death and resurrection, and birth. Having a baby is an experience akin to dying and rising again. At those times we stand right at the boundaries of life, and it can feel as though there is a hair's breadth between death and new life. It is this image that Peter chooses to use to describe what has happened to us as Christians. Through Jesus' resurrection God gives birth to us again. He recreates us into a hope that lives and breathes just as we do. The realm in which we now live is marked by living hope, not life-sapping despair. For the New Testament writers hope was not an emotion, as it often is today, but a reality. This living hope exists whether we feel hopeful or not and is another marker of the risen life we now live.

Concluding reflections

One thing that stands out in nearly all of the references to Jesus' resurrection in the Epistles is that it is simply not possible to say that the resurrection of Jesus is a distant historical event that has little or no impact on our day-to-day lives. Quite the opposite in fact: in the Epistles we see that Jesus' resurrection:

- changes how we think about the future and acts as a guarantee that there is more to life than this world and this age;
- changes how we think about God and reveals something about God's nature as a God who has both the power and the willingness to raise someone from the dead;
- changes how we think about our identity, which is transformed now 'in Christ', since we have died and been raised to new life with him;

and, probably most important of all

- changes how we do everything that we do.

Christ's risen existence transforms us and our lives and the only response to this is to live differently, to live lives infused by resurrection values of reconciliation, freedom and hope.

Almost inevitably, when the authors of the Epistles talk about resurrection they talk in ideals, of what ought to be the case now that Jesus is alive. There are other places in the Epistles where even Paul is realistic and recognizes that ideals and reality do not always match up. Nevertheless, I think he is right to set out those ideals and to encourage us to raise our sights high. There is an adage that goes 'aim for the sky and you might hit the top of a tree'. This is the ultimate aiming for the sky. Missing should not make us lose heart but should reinforce our vision of what might be. We live before the ending of the world. The world in which we live will never be perfect in this age. This does not mean, however, that there cannot be glimmers of end times perfection right now. People of the resurrection are called to strive for those glimmers but always to bear in mind that we do so in order to allow Christ's glory to shine into the world, a glory that shines best through cracked and flawed vessels.

6

AT THE RIGHT HAND
OF GOD

The Ascension

Introduction

Of the four events – death, resurrection ascension and Pentecost – the ascension is the least celebrated. One of the reasons for this is that the day upon which the churches celebrate the festival is 40 days after Easter, and so always on a Thursday, not a Sunday. This is the least of the problems, however. It is easy to see the ascension as a slight dip between the high points of Easter and Pentecost. Easter and Pentecost are moments of great celebration, whereas the ascension recalls the final goodbye of the earthly Jesus. Since Good Friday is the day on which we remember the great loss of Jesus at his death, it can feel hard to be ready to say farewell yet again.

An even greater problem is the view of the world represented by the ascension – even its name suggests problems. The ascension recalls Jesus going upwards into heaven. This comes from a time in which people thought that heaven lay directly above earth and that reaching it meant going up. We now live in a world where people go 'up' everyday, up above the clouds – and more rarely up beyond the earth's atmosphere – and we all know that heaven is not to be found spatially above earth. How then do we talk about the ascension if we no longer have the same view of the world as the earliest Christians?

This chapter explores both what Acts tells us of the story of the ascension and why the ascension is important for the way in which we view Christ and ourselves. In my view, the ascension is not a low point between the resurrection and Pentecost but is an equally high point in the Christian year that deserves a much greater celebration than we normally give it.

When he had said this, as they were watching, he was lifted up, and a cloud took him out of their sight. While he was going and they were gazing up toward heaven, suddenly two men in white robes stood by them. They said, 'Men of Galilee, why do you stand looking up toward heaven? This Jesus, who has been taken up from you into heaven, will come in the same way as you saw him go into heaven.'

Acts 1.9–11

For further reading: Acts 1

A favourite sermon illustration for Ascensiontide is the letting go of lots of helium balloons. I have been at numerous ascension services that have had some form of balloons included in them. At these services I have often found myself wondering whether using balloons as an illustration hinders rather than helps our understanding of the ascension because the balloons float upwards, though clearly not to heaven, and then run out of helium and come down again, or get snagged in a tree and pop. Does this really communicate the essence of the ascension?

In some ways we, like the disciples, have become fixated on the upwards movement of Jesus. The two men in white robes, who are normally taken to be angels, ask the disciples why they are standing looking upwards. Today we stand looking upwards quizzically, no longer clear about why we are looking up but doing so anyway. The point that the two men make to the disciples is, for me, the clue to helping us to understand the ascension properly today. The point is not so much that Jesus has gone upwards but that he has gone. The direction of his movement is not as important as his absence.

At ascension we celebrate the great divine absence, which is a vital ingredient in our call to mission. I don't mean by this that God has abandoned us but that, if Jesus were still on earth in his risen existence, we would probably leave him to it. We might stand on the edge making admiring noises but it would be hard to join in. Who could feel confident to make disciples, to baptize or to teach Jesus' commandments if Jesus were likely to appear at any moment? Who would listen to our proclamation of the good news if they could hear it from Jesus instead?

I remember when I was a student I moved from a church in which there was lots and lots of help to one that had very little indeed. They begged me to teach the Sunday school and I blanched. Sunday school is not something I have ever been particularity good at, but they were desperate, really, really desperate. So I did it. As I suspected, I wasn't very good but that didn't matter hugely. What mattered was that I did it. Then another member of the congregation noticed how much I was struggling by myself and offered to help me. We discovered that together we made a rather good team. None of this would have happened, however, without the desperation of absence.

Jesus' absence is the vital link in God's foolhardy plan to show his love for the world. First he sent his son, who could have died in the animals' feeding trough in the stable or at any point along the way before he did actually die on the cross. Then, having raised him from the dead, he leaves us to finish what Jesus began. It is the riskiest plan possible, but bizarrely – largely because it was God's plan – it has worked. There is no harm in reminding ourselves, however, how essential we are to this. God still entrusts the world and everyone in it, whom he loves so much, to our care. There is no one except us to do it. God waits for us to realize the need and to fill it. It is not a sensible suggestion, but a better sermon illustration for ascension might be for the leader of the service to walk out and leave the congregation alone. This might get closer to communicating the real message of Ascensiontide.

❧

But filled with the Holy Spirit, he gazed into heaven and saw the glory of God and Jesus standing at the right hand of God. 'Look,' he said, 'I see the heavens opened and the Son of Man standing at the right hand of God!'

Acts 7.55–6

For further reading: Acts 7.1–60

We have noticed already the spatial disadvantage that we have when it comes to conceiving of heaven. For us, up can no longer communicate heaven to us because we know that spatially and physically above us lies the universe not the heavenly realms. This is not an insuperable problem. I am no scientist (by any stretch of the imagination) but I believe from those who are that there are now increasing views of the world as been multi-dimensional. In the view of those who lived at the time of the New Testament things could only exist up, down, left, right, forwards or backwards, but now it is possible to understand the universe in a different way, which is far more complex than most human beings can grasp. Heaven could exist in a way that transcends our three-dimensional view of the world – though we might still need to develop language that communicates this and doesn't just fall back on old three-dimensional ways of describing things.

Stephen's vision of Christ is important not because it answers this question but because it tells us what happened to Christ after ascension. For us ascension is about absence but for Christ it is about homecoming. One of the most common descriptions of the ascended Christ is that he is now at the right hand of God (Romans 8.34; Ephesians 1.20; Colossians 3.1; Hebrews 10.12; 12.2; 1 Peter 3.22) in the heavenly realms. This is highly significant. The right hand of God was the location of his power (see, for example, Psalm 48.10: 'Your right hand is filled with victory') and was the promised location for God's chosen Davidic leader (see Psalm 110.1 'The LORD says to my lord, "Sit at my right hand until I make your enemies your footstool."'). What was also important is that in most of the New Testament references, Jesus is sitting at the right hand of the father. There are numerous references in Jewish literature to angelic beings around the throne of God and discussion of whether they were or were not allowed either to sit down in God's company at all or, in particular cases, to sit on God's throne.

Given this discussion of whether angels could sit in God's presence, the language used of the ascended Christ becomes even more significant since it seems that he was not only sitting in God's company but sitting on God's own throne – not on a separate throne to the side of him (this becomes particularly clear in Revelation where the lamb is described as being in the centre of the throne, Revelation 7.17). Jesus' ascension reveals his true nature not only as God's son but as the only being worthy, right now, to sit on the throne with God. This tradition – and its importance for what it was saying about Jesus – makes it all the more odd that Jesus is standing here not sitting as he is elsewhere. Suggestions that have been made are that either he is standing to welcome Stephen before the throne of God or that he is standing as an advocate of Stephen before God's throne.

This second option seems to me to be the more likely and picks up the theme of Jesus being our advocate in the heavenly realms that can be found in 1 John 2.1 ('But if anyone does sin, we have an advocate with the Father, Jesus Christ the righteous'), which may mirror the Spirit's advocacy on earth. The resurrected and ascended Jesus now represents us from his position on God's throne itself. He is no longer present on earth but brings us and our concerns directly to God. He is no longer physically present on earth but brings embodied humanity into heaven and makes us present before God on his throne.

❦

But each of us was given grace according to the measure of Christ's gift. Therefore it is said, 'When he ascended on high he made captivity itself a captive; he gave gifts to his people.' (When it says, 'He ascended,' what does it mean but that he had also descended (into the lower parts of the earth? He who descended is the same one who ascended far above all the heavens, so that he might fill all things.)

Ephesians 4.7–10

For further reading: Ephesians 4.1–12 (you may also like to read Psalm 68.1–18)

I have a study on the top floor of the house and there are days when it feels as though I spend most of the day on the stairs going up and coming down, then going up again and coming down again. Some days it gets so bad (particularly if I stop on the way to do something) that I forget which direction I was going in when I first set off. It can feel as though this passage is a bit like that: Jesus ascended, descended, descended and ascended. Until we begin to wonder where he has been and where he is going. It's actually a lot simpler than it seems, fortunately!

This passage only refers to one descent and one ascent, but it is done in a slightly clumsy order. The argument is that if Jesus is said to have ascended then it must mean that at some point before then he descended (that is, you have to have gone down before you can go up) and, very importantly, the one who came down – the Jesus of the incarnation – is the very same Jesus as the one who went up and now gives us gifts. The implication of the passage is that there were some people who were saying that the Jesus who was human and lived among us was not the same being as the one who has now ascended and is giving gifts to the Church. There is always a danger that we might imply this. There is a preference among some people to talk about the incarnate Jesus as Jesus, and the ascended Christ, as Christ. There is a value in it because we are clearer about what side of the ascension we are talking about; the danger, however, is that we imply that they are different beings. As the passages from the book of Hebrews below make clear, it is precisely because the Jesus at the right hand of God was the incarnate Jesus that we can have confidence in God's presence. The Jesus who ascended has to be the same Jesus as the one who descended or the gifts that we are given are devalued.

In fact it is the gifts that provide a clue to what Paul is talking about in this passage. Ephesians is one of those epistles that oozes a knowledge of the Old Testament but this is one of only two direct – or semi-direct – quotations from it. Verse 8 ('When he ascended on high he made captivity itself a captive; he gave gifts to his people.') is a partial quotation of Psalm 68.18, which talks of God's victory parade after a battle with God's enemies, when he went up onto a high mountain so that everyone could see him, leading his captives and receiving gifts from everyone he met as was his due (as all the ancient kings and emperors did). This is a semi-quotation because Paul uses Psalm 68.18 to show how different things are now in Christ. Jesus brings in his wake not captives – but captivity itself. He has defeated captivity, one of God's greatest enemies, and now does not look to receive gifts but to give them out. Jesus' glorious, ascended victory is expressed not in receiving but in giving gifts. The ascended Christ pours out his generosity on his followers just as he did when he was on earth, enabling us to continue the task that he set us. It is easy to get hung up on the significance of the particular gifts listed here in Ephesians but to do so would be to miss the point. What is important is not exactly what is given but that the gifts are given at all. We have come to a victory feast at which we discover the guest of honour giving out presents rather than receiving them. These are gifts that, by rights, should belong to him – we should then cherish them all the more because of this.

Let the same mind be in you that was in Christ Jesus, who, though he was in the form of God, did not regard equality with God as something to be exploited, but emptied himself, taking the form of a slave, being born in human likeness. And being found in human form, he humbled himself and became obedient to the point of death – even death on a cross. Therefore God also highly exalted him and gave him the name that is above every name, so that at the name of Jesus every knee should bend, in heaven and on earth and under the earth, and every tongue should confess that Jesus Christ is Lord, to the glory of God the Father.

Philippians 2.5–11

For further reading: Philippians 2.1–11

If the resurrection seems remote from our everyday lives, the ascension feels even further away. We noted with Acts 1.9–11 that the impact of the ascension on the disciples was that of absence. The other side of the coin, see among other places in Acts 7.55–6, is the affirmation of Christ's divinity in heaven seated on God's throne. Surely, though, that is just to do with him and nothing to do with us? Does it affect our worship of him but little else? In Philippians 2, Paul answers these questions with a resounding no. Jesus' descent to earth, life among us and subsequent ascent back to heaven are to be to us the model for our own way of life. Philippians 2.5–11 must be understood in terms of its opening statement (and in fact also in terms of verses 1–4, which are all about how we act towards one another). The much more famous 2.6–11, sometimes called the Philippians hymn, only makes sense if we understand it in terms of Paul's exhortations about selflessness and humility.

It is not too clear what the best translation for verse 5 should be. The gist is clear – this is what we should be like – but exactly what it means is harder. Paul is talking here about the way in which we think or our view of the world. It is not so much about what we do as about what goes on in our heads. The other notoriously difficult word to translate describes Jesus: 'he did not consider consider equality with God and thing to be ???'. The NRSV opted for 'exploited', whereas many other translations go for 'grasped'. The problem is that the word can either mean seized (that is, by someone who did not have it before) or held onto (that is, used for one's own advantage). It is clear that the second option must be meant here. Jesus already had equality with God so the meaning must be more around holding tight and making the most of it. I wonder whether 'clutched' might be a good alternative. It is a word that describes a lot of toddlers' behaviour. They do both kinds of grasping. They snatch something from their fellow children and then hold tight to it, clutching it close to their chest lest anyone else should get any benefit from it. If we are honest, it's not only toddlers who do this. As we get older we just become more adept at not appearing to do it.

Paul encourages the Philippians to have the same frame of mind as Jesus whose outlook was not limited by what he could clutch and keep to himself but by his outpouring of himself in love for the world. Christians are sometimes worried about being taken advantage of. In a Christ-like mindset this is simply not possible. Generous self-outpouring cannot be taken advantage of because it is given out freely and undeservedly – you don't have to need it in order to receive it. It is this model that we are called to follow and are reminded that in the topsy-turvy world of the kingdom of God those who give up their rights and pour themselves out, gain back far, far more than they could ever imagine. This model of outpouring is not an additional requirement for Christians but the essence of Christian life and faith. This is the frame of mind, the outlook, the way of life that we follow, modelled for us by the risen and ascended Christ.

༒

Since, then, we have a great high priest who has passed through the heavens, Jesus, the Son of God, let us hold fast to our confession. For we do not have a high priest who is unable to sympathize with our weaknesses, but we have one who in every respect has been tested as we are, yet without sin. Let us therefore approach the throne of grace with boldness, so that we may receive mercy and find grace to help in time of need.

Hebrews 4.14–16

For further reading: Hebrews 4.1–16 (and also Leviticus 16 if you would like to read more about the High Priest)

Human empathy is a powerful thing. On one level it ought to make no difference whether a person in a public role is like us or not, so long as they do a good job, and yet it does. If there is no one like us in terms of gender, or age, or background, or a particular group, it can feel as though we are not really represented. It ought not to make a difference, but it does and the author to the Hebrews knows this.

The majority of his argument in chapter 4 is an encouragement to keep the faith, to hold on and to be firm whatever life throws up. The climax of his argument can be found in 4.14–16 where he reminds his readers why this is not only possible but important to do. We hold fast to what we have already agreed to (our confession) for two reasons: we have a High Priest who has passed through the heavens and who is able to sympathize with our weaknesses. These two reasons represent the two aspects of the risen Christ's identity – heavenly and earthly.

The particular role of the High Priest was attached to the Day of Atonement when he alone could enter the Holy of Holies in the temple to make atonement on behalf of the sins of the people. Only the High Priest had the right to do this because only he was qualified to stand in the presence of God. The earthly High Priest represented the people before God on earth in the place – the Holy of Holies – where God was present from time to time. Our High Priest – Jesus – has not passed through the courts of the temple but through the courts of heaven and intercedes permanently (not just on the Day of Atonement nor before a God who is only sometimes present) on behalf of the people. We can be confident then that Jesus' intercessions on our behalf reach God directly.

The other aspect of Jesus' identity is his humanity. Our confidence here stems from the fact that Jesus knows and sympathizes with everything we go through because he has been there himself. Jesus has suffered just as we do. He was tempted just like us. He understands what it is like to be human and can speak on our behalf. Just as we feel better knowing that someone like us represents us in human institutions, so we can also be confident that someone who has experienced human life in all its forms represents us in heaven.

It is Jesus' ascension that bears our humanity right to the throne of God and it is this in which we can now have confidence. As a result of this, we have permanent access, through prayer, to God's throne and the author reminds us that we should make the most of it. We can approach

God in prayer knowing that he will be constantly, generously and unstintingly on our side as a result of Jesus, the risen and ascended High Priest. Our relationship with God is now a little like having a relative or close friend working for the Queen or the Prime Minister who will guarantee you an audience whenever you want or need one. Imagine having such an access but never using it. This would be like having access to God opened for us by Jesus but never or rarely praying. We have been given that access – so why not use it?

Therefore, since we are surrounded by so great a cloud of witnesses, let us also lay aside every weight and the sin that clings so closely, and let us run with perseverance the race that is set before us, looking to Jesus the pioneer and perfecter of our faith, who for the sake of the joy that was set before him endured the cross, disregarding its shame, and has taken his seat at the right hand of the throne of God.

Hebrews 12.1–2

For further reading: Hebrews 12.1–14

I have never been very good at running but I have always wished that I was. There is something magnetic about the sheer physical stamina and determination needed to run a marathon. The idea of pushing your body to its limits and of striving as hard as you can has an odd appeal, to which the thousands of participators in the different marathons and fun runs that take place every year bear witness. Running was a metaphor with which the original readers of Hebrews would have been all too aware. Racing was the first event in the great pentathlon of the panhellenic games and for many years was the only athletics event at the Ancient Greek Olympic games.

The image being used here by the author is clearly a long-distance race. The reference to a great cloud of witnesses implies that we are to imagine an amphitheatre, packed with spectators who have all run the race in the past (and to whom we are introduced in chapter 11, from Abel to Rahab). Inspired by them and the fact that they have now gathered round to cheer us on, we persevere, break through the pain barrier and run on. In order to do this we need to divest ourselves (the Greek word can also be used of getting undressed) of anything that will make the going tougher. Again the words that are used to describe what we are to take off are immensely evocative. We are to take off anything that is an impediment (that will trip us up) and the sin that entangles us (again the image is of things that wrap around us and so inhibit our ability to run). This will enable us to focus all the more on the race before us. We are inspired by the surrounding crowd of witnesses, but our sight must be fixed clearly on Jesus who, the image used here implies, has run the race before us and is waiting for us at the finishing line, urging us on to its completion. Although it is not stated explicitly here in the way that it was in Hebrews 4.14–16, again it is implied that we can trust Jesus to be the goal of our race not only because he has run the course ahead of us but because he has finished it and is willing us to do the same.

Shifting the image a little, the author of Hebrews goes on to talk about Jesus as the pioneer and perfecter of our faith. Not only was Jesus the first one to go by this route, he also did it in the fastest time. We must follow in his footsteps and aim to keep up with how he ran the race.

One more time we discover, then, that the ascension of Jesus did not make him remote and far distant from our lives but offered to us a role model for us to emulate. As with all good role models, Jesus is sufficiently far above us to give us something to aim for but has shared enough of our experience for us to trust that he knows what it is like. It is widely acknowledged that the best people to talk to addicts are ex-addicts, who can offer aspiration interwoven with experience. The ascended Jesus offers to us the same thing: the aspiration of standing in the presence of God interwoven with the knowledge that he has also stood where we stand. The ascended Jesus stands before us, calling us onwards and encouraging us to persevere no matter how hard it is, because he has gone this way before us.

Concluding reflections

The ascension can feel even more remote from us than the resurrection, but in fact it shapes our lives as Christians at least as much as, if not more than, the resurrection. The resurrection transforms us, our relationships and the world around us but the ascension gives us both the motivation to act and a blueprint for how to do it. Without the absence of Jesus, we may still have been trailing around after him waiting to be told what to do. We need the ascension to make us act but we also need the ascended Jesus to act as role model for us. As we have seen, so many of the passages that talk about Jesus being on the right hand of God use Jesus as the model for Christian character. As Christians we should have our eyes fixed firmly on the ascended Jesus who has gone this way before us and,

- like him, let go of all those things we clutch to ourselves, pouring ourselves out in love for the world;
- make the most of our permanent welcome before the throne of God in prayer confident that, because of him, we will be always welcome;
- like him persevere to the end.

Christian character is Christ-like character marked by love, confidence and tenacity. It is this we learn from the risen and ascended Christ who has gone before us in everything that we do.

7

SPIRIT-FILLED LIVES

Pentecost

Introduction

Pentecost is the final – but vital – link in the chain that moves us from a terrified, timid group of disciples before Jesus' death to the powerful, confident proclaimers of good news throughout the whole world. The contrast between the disciples before Jesus' death and after Pentecost could not be greater. Before Jesus' death the disciples struggled to understand who Jesus really was, they failed to stay awake in the garden of Gethsemane, when Jesus needed their company and, at his arrest when he needed them most, they ran away. After Pentecost the disciples spread throughout the world proclaiming the good news of Jesus whatever the cost. They became inspiring and confident communicators, infused with joy and enthusiasm. It is easy to attribute this solely to the coming of the spirit at Pentecost, but to do so would be to misunderstand the chain of events that leads up to this point. Jesus' death destroyed all their expectations about who he was. The resurrection put these expectations back together again in a different order and helped them to understand who Jesus really was. The ascension opened up a space that required them to act and, finally, the coming of the Holy Spirit gave them the ability to do so. Pentecost was a vital link in the chain but not the only one in the disciples' growth towards transformation.

It is worth reminding ourselves that Pentecost was originally a Jewish festival that has become re-infused with importance within Christianity. The reason that there were so many people for Peter to speak to at Pentecost was because they were all in Jerusalem for the feast of Pentecost (Greek name) or Shavuot (Hebrew name). Shavuot was one of the great Jewish harvest festivals at which they also celebrated the giving of the law on Mount Sinai. It had to take place 50 days after the festival of Passover and in certain ways our celebration of the coming of the Holy Spirit patterns the original meaning of the feast. The feast of Passover recalled the people of God's freedom from slavery and Shavuot/Pentecost the giving of the law, which shaped how they served God in that freedom; Easter recalls our freedom from death and sin and Pentecost the giving of the Holy Spirit, which shapes how we serve God in that freedom.

When the day of Pentecost had come, they were all together in one place. And suddenly from heaven there came a sound like the rush of a violent wind, and it filled the entire house where they were sitting. Divided tongues, as of fire, appeared among them, and a tongue rested on each of them. All of them were filled with the Holy Spirit and began to speak in other languages, as the Spirit gave them ability.

Acts 2.1–4

For further reading: Exodus 19.1–25 to be read alongside Acts 2.1–4

One of the feelings that we, as human beings, love is exclusivity. The sense that something is available only to us – or to us and only a few others – makes us feel important, somehow more significant than other people. Advertisers rely on this when they invite us to 'exclusive openings' or 'once-in-a-lifetime deals' Things suddenly become more attractive if people realize that an event only has a few spaces left or that something is a limited edition. Where before we were ambivalent about it, on discovering that we might miss out, we become desperate to acquire it – or at least that is what many advertisers rely on. This is a concept that stretches to religion too. Some of the most powerful cults or sects throughout history have been those that keep inner secrets among their membership, or among an elite of their membership.

If we compare the story of the coming of the Holy Spirit at Pentecost with that of the giving of the law on Mount Sinai, there are some remarkable overlaps. On Mount Sinai there was, among other features, a loud sound like a trumpet (Exodus 19.16) and fire that descended on the mountian; at Pentecost we hear of a sound like a violent wind (which is also reminiscent of Elijah's encounter with God on Mount Horeb in 1 Kings 19.11–12) and of tongues like fire appearing among the disciples. In some ways the giving of the Holy Spirit at Pentecost is another outpouring of God like that at Sinai and is marked by similar characteristics of divine presence, such as wind and fire.

There is, however, one very important difference. When Moses when up Mount Sinai the people were warned twice not to come near (Exodus 19.12 and 21). God's presence was too dangerous for them and could only be encountered by Moses, or Moses and Aaron. The revelation of God in the Old Testament was kept for only a few, special people like Moses, Elijah and Isaiah. All others were kept away lest the revelation prove too much for them. In Acts 2, no one is kept away. The Holy Spirit does not just descend on Peter, or on Peter, James and John but upon all of the people who were gathered there and then, subsequently, on all those who heard and responded to the message. One of the wonderful features of our Christian faith is that nothing is secret or exclusive. Everything is open to everyone. This is a vital strand that runs through the New Testament beginning with the ministry of Jesus, re-enforced here at Pentecost, and again and again in the writings of Paul.

It may be re-enforced but somehow we still struggle to come to terms with it. Christian gatherings of all sorts fall all too easily into exclusivity: where some belong and others do not; where some feel themselves at the centre and others about as unwelcome as they can be. This is one of those places where living Spirit-filled lives is at odds with human instinct. The Holy Spirit continues to pour into our lives, refusing to observe boundaries that pronounce on those who are worthy and those who are not, those who are 'in' and those who are 'out'. The coming of the Holy Spirit at Pentecost flings wide the doors, declaring that all are welcome, that no one is to keep away. We are no longer told, as the Israelites were, 'not to break through to the Lord' (Exodus 19.21) because the Lord breaks through to us over and over again, if only we will let him.

Now there were devout Jews from every nation under heaven living in Jerusalem. And at this sound the crowd gathered and was bewildered, because each one heard them speaking in the native language of each. Amazed

*and astonished, they asked, 'Are not all these who are
speaking Galileans? And how is it that we hear, each of
us, in our own native language?'*

Acts 2.5–8

For further reading: Acts 2.5–13 (and also Genesis
11.1–9)

One of my favourite experiences is being in a service in
which people all say the Lord's Prayer in their own language. Of course, this only works if there are enough
nationalities represented, having only two or three languages just sounds a little odd. I used to teach at a college
in which there were people from many, many nationalities and what struck me every time we did this was that
although you might expect this to be an occasion in which
differences came to the fore, it felt quite the opposite and
was an experience of incredible unity and harmony. The
experience of praying the same prayer to the same God
in languages from all around the world brought us closer
together as the family of God on earth.

We noticed in the previous section how Exodus 19 can
enrich our understanding of the story of the coming of
the Holy Spirit at Pentecost. That, however, is not the
only Old Testament passage that lies behind this passage. There are allusions and quotations from a number
of other passages as well, including Genesis 11.1–9 and
Joel 2.28–30 (we will explore the passage from Joel in the
section that follows this one). The account of the building
of the tower of Babel in Genesis 11.1–9 is one of the more
comic stories from the book of Genesis. Human beings
found a place to live and decided to build a tower with
its top in the heavens, so that they could make a name for
themselves and would not be scattered across the face of

the earth. To celebrate their own greatness they built an enormous tower, so big that it reached the heavens, but from God's perspective it was still so small that he had to come down in order to be able to see it. They built the tower to ensure that they could entrench their power and not be scattered throughout the earth: God scattered them anyway and caused them to speak different languages to limit their power.

Here in Acts we have a story with certain similarities (including people from all over the world speaking different languages and God coming down to them) but the outcome is somewhat different. Here people from all over the world came to Jerusalem and God came down to them as before but this time the experience does not scatter them but brings them closer together. This time they find themselves able not only to understand people who normally speak different languages from themselves but also to encounter God as well. The tower of Babel brought division and alienation to the world but Pentecost reversed it. The experience at Pentecost is Babel reversed and renewed.

Humanity becomes unified once more not so that we can glory in our own strength but in God's, not so that we can make a name for ourselves but so that God's name might be made known throughout the world. Though today we cannot necessarily understand when someone else speaks – even when they speak the same language as us – the experience of the sending of the Holy Spirit should mean that we are no longer alienated from each other. When we gather to proclaim God's deeds of power and to pray, we have a deep and lasting unity grounded in God. The action of the Holy Spirit draws us together in unity – sometimes even despite our words.

৻৵৵

*But Peter, standing with the eleven, raised his voice
and addressed them, 'Men of Judea and all who live in
Jerusalem, let this be known to you, and listen to what
I say. Indeed, these are not drunk, as you suppose, for
it is only nine o'clock in the morning. No, this is what
was spoken through the prophet Joel: "In the last days
it will be, God declares, that I will pour out my Spirit
upon all flesh, and your sons and your daughters shall
prophesy, and your young men shall see visions, and
your old men shall dream dreams . . ."'*

Acts 2.14–17

For further reading: Acts 2.14–41 (and Joel 2.23–32)

I've mentioned already my family's love of bad jokes and
I feel a few more coming on. 'How do you know you
have an elephant in your fridge?' – footprints in the but-
ter. 'How do you know there's an elephant in your bed?'
– she has an E on her pyjamas. 'How do you know that
we are in the end times?' You'll be relieved to know that
the answer is nothing to do with elephants. We know that
we are in the end times when long-prophesied events for
the end-times begin to be fulfilled.

One of the most influential prophecies about the end
times in the Old Testament is Joel's prophecy about
prophets and dreamers that Peter cites here. Joel's prophecy opens with a promise of utter destruction, which will
be followed by a time of plenty in which everything that
has been stripped from the land will be restored. As a part
of that Israel will know that God, the only God, is in the

midst of them. There can be no mistake that Peter chose this particular prophecy with which to begin his powerful speech in Jerusalem. It seems to be a powerful affirmation of who he now knows Jesus to be. In the book of Joel the promise that there would be a time of prophesying and dreaming dreams, is immediately preceded by the promise that they will know that God – the only God – was in their midst (Joel 2.27). There is hardly a better description of Jesus' incarnation than that he was in the midst of Israel as God, the only God.

Also important was that, in some people's minds at least, the period of the last few centuries before Jesus' birth was marked by the lack of prophecy, a lack that, people believed, would be reversed at the end times. The use of this prophecy here may signal not only a significant moment in the world's history but that the end times were now at hand – a period that, as we have seen already, began with Jesus' resurrection but has not yet come to an end. In a speech resonant with prophecy, Peter announces that these longed-for days are now upon us. This connection may, at first glance, appear odd since Peter was not particularly talking about the future. His speech was far more concerned with the present. What this does is draw us more deeply into an understanding of Old Testament prophecy. Old Testament prophecy was only sometimes about the future; it was much more often concerned with speaking God's words into the present. A true prophet perceived the things of God (whether past, present or future) and proclaimed them to all around them.

Pentecost is a moment, par excellence, of prophetic outpouring. Peter and the rest of the disciples have perceived God as never before and are proclaiming him at the tops of their voices in many different languages. Never before has Israel had such an outpouring of prophetic activity as happened on that day of Pentecost. There is no doubt in Peter's mind – or indeed in the author of Acts, Luke's mind – that the time prophesied by Joel has already begun. The longed-for future marked by God's presence in their midst and the return of prophetic witness to the land is now before them. Now is the time and it must be shouted from the rooftops. Filled by the Spirit, Peter and the other disciples for the first time understood fully not only who Jesus was but what this meant for the world. Filled by the Spirit, they were transformed into confident, proclaimers of God's good news. The end times that Peter so clearly identified are still upon us and we are called now, as then, to be Spirit-filled prophets in the world: perceiving and proclaiming God's presence and saving action in our midst.

When it was evening on that day, the first day of the week, and the doors of the house where the disciples had met were locked for fear of the Jews, Jesus came and stood among them and said, 'Peace be with you.' After he said this, he showed them his hands and his side. Then the disciples rejoiced when they saw the Lord. Jesus said to them again, 'Peace be with you. As the Father has sent me, so I send you.' When he had said this, he breathed on them and said to them, 'Receive the Holy Spirit. If you forgive the sins of any, they are forgiven them; if you retain the sins of any, they are retained.'

John 20.19–23

There is something elegant about the passing on of a baton in a relay race. It is great to watch a well-trained relay team at the top of their game warming up, running alongside each other for a few moments before fluidly and skilfully passing the baton from one to another so that, as one athlete slows down and completes their part, the other speeds up and runs their own particular leg of the race. If a good handover is elegant, a bad one is excruciating: a stuttering rhythm or slipped grip can ruin a relay no matter how fast the next athlete runs.

There is often a huge amount of discussion about whether John's account of the giving of the Spirit is of the same event or different from the one in Luke's account in Acts. There are certainly some differences the most obvious of which is that Jesus gives his Spirit to the disciples directly himself, rather than more remotely after his ascension. What I think is important here is what this tells us about John's view of the passing on of the baton of Jesus' ministry. In Luke, Jesus gave the disciples a commission but there was a gap between the giving of the commission and them doing it. In Luke, the giving of the Spirit focuses our attention upon the enabling action of the Spirit.

In John, there is no gap. We receive the task directly from Jesus ('As my Father sent me, so I send you', John 20.21) but we also receive the Spirit directly from him too (John 20.22). In John the task, and ability and authority to do it are intertwined. Jesus sends the disciples, just as he has been sent. He gives them the Spirit directly and at the same time imbues them with divine authority to act. Part of the significance of Jesus' statement about the forgiveness of sins ('If you forgive the sins of any, they are forgiven them; if you retain the sins of any, they are retained', John 20.23) is divine authority. God was the one who had authority to forgive sins, an authority that was passed to Jesus and now is passed on to the disciples.

In John there is a single chain from Father to Son to dis-

ciples, just as in the best changeovers in relay races a single fluid motion transfers the baton into new keeping. Of
course, the fluidity of the handover is equally dependent
not only the the runner who hands on the baton but on
the one who receives it. A perfect delivery can be spoiled
by the one who receives it. John's account of the giving of
the Spirit reminds us of the importance of the task deliv-
ered into our care. We are now the bearers of the sacred
mission passed from God to Jesus to the earliest disciples
and now onwards to us. We receive both the task and the
Spirit who will enable us to act, but how well we receive
them is up to us.

✾

*For all who are led by the Spirit of God are children of
God. For you did not receive a spirit of slavery to fall
back into fear, but you have received a spirit of adoption. When we cry, 'Abba! Father!' it is that very Spirit
bearing witness with our spirit that we are children of
God, and if children, then heirs, heirs of God and joint
heirs with Christ – if, in fact, we suffer with him so that
we may also be glorified with him.*

Romans 8.14–17

For further reading:Romans 8.1–17

I remember that moment in my childhood when modern
language versions of the Bible became more widely used
and we switched from talking about the Holy Ghost to
talking about the Holy Spirit. I also remember a certain
level of bemusement when I was told that the phrase 'the
Holy Ghost' was confusing so it was much better to talk

about the Holy Spirit, which was much clearer and easier to understand. I didn't dare show myself up by saying that I had no real idea what either of them meant. True, Holy Ghost had resonances of ghouls and things that go bump in the night but surely Holy Spirit wasn't without its problems either, with its implications of the spirit world or alcoholic beverages? Nevertheless, since everyone else seemed so clear about what it meant I decided that the only course of action was to keep my mouth shut and nod in the right places when people talked about the Holy Spirit. Perhaps it was inevitable that I would become a New Testament scholar, because the more I study Paul the more I realize that it isn't just me who has problems with the Holy Spirit. Luke may have a relatively clear understanding of the Holy Spirit but in Paul it is much more complicated.

This chapter of Romans is an excellent example of this. One of the problems for understanding the Spirit is working out how it relates to God, to Jesus and to us. Verse 9 of chapter 8, a few verses before this passage, says: 'But you are not in the flesh; you are in the Spirit, since the Spirit of God dwells in you. Anyone who does not have the Spirit of Christ does not belong to him.' Here we have three references to the 'Spirit': one that talks about being 'in the Spirit', one that talks about the Spirit of God and another that talks about the Spirit of Christ. All three seem to refer to the Spirit in very slightly different ways. We are in the realm of the Spirit (as opposed to the realm of the flesh) if we have the Spirit of God and belonging to Christ involves having the Spirit of Christ. Add to this Romans 8.16, which says that God's Spirit joins with our spirit to bear witness that we are God's children, and it all begins to feel a little complicated.

Precisely how do all of these relate to each other? Is the Spirit of God the same as the Spirit of Christ? Which of these is The Spirit? And how does that Spirit relate to our own spirit? This is all made even more difficult – if that is possible – by the fact that in Greek there are no capital letters, as there are in English, to differentiate between The Spirit and our spirit, our English translators have added the capital letters in an attempt to make it easier for us to negotiate through this complex territory.

A close reading of Paul makes it clear that Spirit/spirit language is even more important than we might otherwise realize. We noticed in the passages about resurrection that Jesus' resurrection ushered in a new way of being, which brought forward into the present some aspects of living in the end times. We live now in a reality that reveals glimmers of a world newly created by God. This reality is, in Paul's language, the realm of the Spirit. If we are 'in Christ' we live in the realm of the Spirit, rather than the realm of the flesh, and live lives governed by Spirit principles rather than flesh principles. Thus we are 'in the Spirit' and infused by the Spirit, our own spirits imbued by God's Spirit respond 'spiritwise' to the world and everything in it. In short, our view of the Spirit is often too narrow and closely defined to something that is 'other' than us. At the resurrection and Pentecost, God's realm – the realm of the Spirit – broke into our world and calls us to live 'spiritwise'. This involves not just something that is other than us but describes the whole of our existence.

∽☜❀☞∼

For the creation waits with eager longing for the revealing of the children of God ... We know that the whole creation has been groaning in labour pains until now; and not only the creation, but we ourselves, who

*have the first fruits of the Spirit, groan inwardly while
we wait for adoption, the redemption of our bodies ...
Likewise the Spirit helps us in our weakness; for we
do not know how to pray as we ought, but that very
Spirit intercedes with sighs too deep for words. And
God, who searches the heart, knows what is the mind
of the Spirit, because the Spirit intercedes for the saints
according to the will of God.*

Romans 8.19, 22–3, 26–7

For further reading: Romans 8.18–27

Throughout much of this book we have been in the territory of ideals. These are the ideals of big theological ideas
like resurrection existence, life 'in Christ' and being transformed by the Holy Spirit. These ideals talk about what a
world transformed by Christ's resurrection might be like.
What many of the passages we have explored have not
done, however, is reminded us of the 'not yet' part of
our existence as Christians. Many of the New Testament
writers are keen to fix our eyes on the vision of what the
resurrection might mean and how this will affect the way
in which we live our lives. So much so, in fact, that if we
were not careful we could easily feel guilty about the way
in which our lives don't quite match up to the glorious
vision we are offered. It is, frankly, hard to live the whole
of our lives infused by the Spirit and inspired by Christ
– even the holiest of people would struggle after a while.

It seems right, therefore, to end our reflections with
a passage that acknowledges the 'between-ness' of our
present lives. We do, now, live in a world in which there
are glimmers of end times existence, but they are only
glimmers – here one moment and gone the next. Alongside this lies a reality that is still waiting for the end times

to happen, in which the realm of the Spirit competes with the realm of this age, in which what we yearn to do 'in Christ' often fails and leaves us disappointed. This passage from Romans 8 reminds us of what we still wait for. The whole of creation waits for that glorious moment in the future when the old will pass away in entirety and the new will come. Until that moment comes, we live between the old and the new. Torn between our vision of the world as God intended it to be and the world as it is, between an existence shaped only by Christ and one shaped by the cares and concerns of this world.

Before we give up in despair, however, Paul reminds us that we are not alone in this 'between' existence because we who are in the Spirit have the Spirit with us who groans just as we do. The NRSV does not help particularly here since its translation uses different words for what we do (groan, v. 23) and what the Spirit does (sighs, v. 26) though both come from the same root in Greek. We do not need to find the words, therefore, to articulate the agonies and frustrations of our 'in between' existence because God's own Spirit is here with us, groaning just like we do and in doing so speaking into the very heart of God.

The Spirit is not just an ideal that we try, and fail, to live up to, but is a part of our life as it is now. Just when we are about to give up, groaning in frustration we discover the Spirit alongside us, groaning too and communicating our deeply felt emotions to God. The Spirit draws us on to where we might be but also meets us where we are and conveys to God everything about who we are and what we do. In characteristic divine form God calls us onwards to places we never dreamed of being but also drops back and walks with us on the way.

Concluding reflections

One of the great values of Luke's account of the death, resurrection and ascension of Jesus and the coming of the Holy Spirit, is that he splits them down and enables us to look at each one in turn. As we do so we appreciate the significance of each of these events. The problem of doing this is that it implies that they are four separate events, unconnected from each other. The value of exploring the Spirit through eyes other than just Luke's is that it allows us to put the pieces together again and to comprehend the seamless whole that occurs in the dying, rising and ascending of Christ and descending of the Spirit. John reminds us that with the Spirit Jesus hands on to us directly the task that he was sent to do by the Father and Paul argues that being 'in Christ' is to be filled by the Spirit, to live in the Spirit and to find our own spirits at one with God's.

Resurrection existence is spirit-filled and spirit-led existence. The world to come is a world governed not by earthly concerns but by spiritual concerns. The resurrection pulled the world of the Spirit – at least in part – into our own world. The resurrection allowed us to live the Spirit-filled lives that became possible at Pentecost. These four events (death, resurrection, ascension and coming of the Holy Spirit) are closely interwoven and, although we can see their individual threads, they should not really be separated too far from each other. The Spirit continues to explode into our lives just as it did with the earliest disciples, transforming us, helping us to be the people that God wants us to be, groaning with us with sounds that reach deep into the heart of God and drawing us more fully into this risen existence.

EPILOGUE

The Spirit of Easter is one that stands at the very heart of our Christian faith. Not only does it tell us about Christ and what happened to him almost 2,000 years ago but it also tells us about us and who we are as Christians. If we believe that Jesus rose from the dead, this is not merely a concept with which we can agree or disagree but something that deeply affects who we are.

Not long ago, at dinner, one of my daughters asked a question that, in my view, puts into words somewhat beautifully the meaning of our resurrection existence. In the midst of the hurly burly of serving and eating dinner, she suddenly said: 'How does Jesus make us real?' Then as my husband and I reached for an answer she continued, 'Does he draw us first and then colour us in?' This, to me, is a wonderful description of the resurrection life. First Jesus draws us, both in the sense of drawing us to him but also in the sense of re-creating and re-figuring us anew into a Christ-like existence; he then proceeds to colour us in. Our continued life in Christ is the way in which he colours us in. There we become more and more Christ-like, increasingly shaped by him until, in our resurrection bodies, the whole of our being is infused with the things of the Spirit and Christ's resurrected life becomes not just a part, but the whole of who we are.

This transformative 'colouring-in' is not just for our

own benefit. It is for the good of the whole created order. In 1 Corinthians 15.45 Paul draws the contrast between Adam and Christ: Adam, he says, was made alive; whereas Christ makes life. If we are in Christ, we become like him. If we are in Christ we are called to become life-givers, life-breathers, life-makers. We become people who bear resurrection with us wherever we go. To return briefly to R.S. Thomas's poem, we wait for him to come, as we have always known he would, and discover as the whole of our being overflows with him as a chalice would the sea, that 'this risen existence' is not just his but ours too.